Senses of Mystery

In this beautifully written book, David E. Cooper uses a gentle walk through a tropical garden – the view of the fields and hills beyond it, the sound of birds, voices and flutes, the reflection of light in water, the play of shadows among the trees and the presence of strange animals – as an opportunity to reflect on experiences of nature and the mystery of existence.

Covering an extensive range of topics, from Daoism to dogs, from gardening to walking, from Zen to Debussy, Cooper succeeds in conveying some deep and difficult philosophical ideas about the meaning of life in an engaging manner, showing how those ideas bear upon the practical question of how we should relate to our world and live our lives.

A thought-provoking and compelling book, *Senses of Mystery* is a triumph of both storytelling and philosophy.

David E. Cooper is Emeritus Professor of Philosophy at Durham University. He has been a Visiting Professor at universities in several countries, including the USA and Sri Lanka. His many books include *The Measure of Things: Humanism, Humility and Mystery*, *A Philosophy of Gardens* and *Convergence with Nature: A Daoist Perspective*.

D1453093

'Cultivation of a sense of mystery has venerable precedent in ancient spiritual traditions, and runs through modern writings on animals, gardens, nature, art, and music. In this personal, humane book, David E. Cooper describes the rhythms and tones of a life shaped by mystery. Gathering the wisdom of sages, composers, gardeners, nature lovers, and others, this book reveals the ways that reflective appreciation of creatures, places, and practices can reveal the depth and mystery that underlies human life.'

Ian James Kidd, *University of Nottingham, UK*

'This world is, indeed, one vast mystery, containing only, here and there, a few scattered islands of human knowledge. Past philosophers have not attended enough to this paradoxical situation, but Cooper now does so. We had better read him.'

Mary Midgley, *Newcastle University, UK*

'*Senses of Mystery* is a superb book – inspiring, beautifully written and packed with insights about a remarkably wide range of topics, from meditative walking to the mystery of existence. I recommend it to anyone who wishes to understand what it means to live in harmony with the natural world.'

Simon P. James, *Durham University, UK*

'This book is a gentle and beautiful evocation of the well lived human life, and the role of familiar practices such as listening to music, walking and gardening in leading us into a transformed appreciation of the everyday world. In Cooper's hands, philosophical reflection has become a spiritual practice.'

Mark Wynn, *University of Leeds, UK*

David E.
Cooper

Senses of Mystery

Engaging with Nature and the
Meaning of Life

Routledge
Taylor & Francis Group

LONDON AND NEW YORK

First published 2018
by Routledge
2 Park Square, Milton Park, Abingdon, Oxon OX14 4RN

and by Routledge
711 Third Avenue, New York, NY 10017

Routledge is an imprint of the Taylor & Francis Group, an informa business

British Library Cataloguing-in-Publication Data
A catalogue record for this book is available from the British Library

Library of Congress Cataloging-in-Publication Data
Names: Cooper, David E. (David Edward), 1942– author.
Title: Senses of mystery : engaging with nature and the meaning of life /
    David E. Cooper.
Description: Abingdon, Oxon ; New York, NY : Routledge is an imprint of the
    Taylor & Francis Group, an Informa Business, [2018] | Includes bibliographical
    references and index.
Identifiers: LCCN 2017009811 (print) | LCCN 2017030048 (ebook) |
    ISBN 9781315112060 (E-book) | ISBN 9781138078727 (hbk : alk. paper) |
    ISBN 9781138078734 (pbk. : alk. paper) | ISBN 9781315112060 (ebk)
Subjects: LCSH: Philosophy of nature. | Life.Classification: LCC BD581 (ebook) |
    LCC BD581 .C6665 2017 (print) | DDC 128—dc23
LC record available at https://lccn.loc.gov/2017009811

ISBN: 978-1-138-07872-7 (hbk)
ISBN: 978-1-138-07873-4 (pbk)
ISBN: 978-1-315-11206-0 (ebk)

Typeset in Joanna MT
by Apex CoVantage, LLC

CONTENTS

ACKNOWLEDGEMENTS

I am very grateful to Simon P. James, Ian James Kidd and Graham Parkes for their warm and helpful remarks on the typescript of this book. I want to thank, too, Peter Cheyne and Guy Bennett-Hunter for commenting on papers on which the book draws. Finally, I am grateful to the ever efficient team at Routledge – Rebecca Shillabeer, Gabrielle Coakeley and Fiona Hudson – with whom it has been a pleasure to work.

1

IN A GARDEN

I am slowly walking down the steps of a garden, alongside a low, moss-covered stone wall beyond which a paddy field stretches towards the hills. It is still light, but soon it will be dark, for here in the tropics – in Sri Lanka – the sun descends quickly. For the moment, rays of sunshine stream through narrow spaces in the thick foliage of the trees. This light is reflected by the surface of the pool that lies at the bottom of the steps, and by the scales of the small red fish that swim just below this surface. As well as the slight plopping sounds made by the fish, I can hear the calls and chatter of birds – crows, parrots, babblers – that briefly stop over in the trees on the way to their roosts. I can also hear the soft sounds of a solitary flute and, still more faintly, the chanting of monks from the temple on a hillside beyond the paddy field.

As I climb back up the steps, the light has already faded. The little world around me is becoming shadowy, its contents indistinct. The sounds, too, have changed. Gone is the calling of the birds, replaced by the incipient rustling and croaking of the creatures that emerge at dusk.

A pleasant early evening stroll? Yes, of course. But on this evening, at least, rather more than that – an occasion for a quiet, undramatic sense of something I want to call a sense of the mystery of things. The gentle walk through the garden, the view of the fields and hills beyond it, the sound of birds, voices and flute, the reflection of light in water, the play of shadows among the trees, the felt presence of strange animals – these come together to provide an opportunity for attunement to the mystery of existence.

Opportunities like this are ones to seek out and cultivate. First, because there is a compelling case for regarding the way of things – reality 'as such', as metaphysicians say – as being mysterious, ineffable. Hence, to experience a sense of mystery, to be attuned to it, is to be in the truth. Second, because it matters to the quality – the flourishing or otherwise – of a human life whether it is led in appreciation of mystery. This is an appreciation that has atrophied in modernity, replaced by a hubristic subordination of everything to human instruments of understanding and measure. This subordination is complicit in some of the moral debacles of modernity – in the devastation of natural environments, for example, and in 'the eternal Treblinka' endured by billions of industrially farmed animals.

'Nothing special', as Zen masters like to put it, is necessary for inviting in and cultivating a sense of mystery. This sense is not a Eureka-like vision of the supernatural. Nor is it the reward for the privations, feats and techniques of ascetic virtuosos and other adepts. Walking, gardening, attention to animals, listening to the sounds of nature and music, watching the play of light and shadows – in none of this is there anything special. But as Zen Buddhists, Daoists and followers of other traditions of wisdom suggest, such simple practices are ones that, mindfully conducted, inspire attunement to mystery.

This book is an elaboration and defence of that suggestion.

2

THE TRUTH OF MYSTERY

INEFFABILITY

There's a compelling case, I just wrote, for regarding the way of things – reality 'as such' – as mysterious, as ineffable. That last word is important, for the mystery of the way of things is not something that we could hope – with more effort and research – to understand and articulate. The way of things is mysterious in the strong sense of being inaccessible to description, at least in literal terms. It is forever resistant to conceptual articulation and understanding. It is, in short, ineffable. Such, famously, is the teaching of the opening verse of the *Daodejing*, which tells us that the way (*dao*) is 'nameless' (Laozi 2003: Ch. 1). It is the teaching, too, of Mahayana Buddhist texts: reality is 'signless' and 'inaccessible to discursive thought' (Conze 1990: 349). It is 'something ineffable coming like this' (Dōgen 1996: Ch. 22).

I want briefly to make the case for mystery, but without the detail and responses to objections that I have supplied in other writings (Cooper 2002). My aim in this book is less to convince readers of the truth of mystery than to communicate, to people already receptive to the idea, some of the ways in which intimations of mystery may be cultivated and integrated into our lives.

Let's return to the garden I walked through and think about some of the terms I used in my description of it. Take, for instance, 'flute', 'temple', 'wall' and 'garden' itself. None of these terms could figure in a description of the world 'in itself', of a world independent of human purposes and perspectives. A hollow length of wood with holes in it is a flute only because of its role in a human practice – music. A pile of stones is a wall only in virtue of its practical function – to separate a garden from a field, say. The point is not that flutes, walls or temples are man-made. In fact it is perfectly possible for a natural site – a cave, say, or a forest clearing – to serve as a temple. A narrow, naturally formed mound of earth could act as a garden wall. The point, rather, is that things count as flutes, walls, temples and the like only in relation to how they are understood and used, how they are regarded from the perspective of human agency. A world without creatures like us – ones who have purposes and perspectives – would be devoid of gardens, flutes, walls and temples.

But, you'll say, it would certainly still contain the trees, rocks, moss and other natural things I came across during my walk in the garden. So the names of these things, you'll insist, will still figure in a description of the world as it is independent of human practices and points of view. Reality, you'll conclude, isn't therefore ineffable.

But what you're saying is unconvincing. Surely it isn't difficult to imagine creatures whose lives – whose perceptions, interests, purposes and practices – are so different from ours that trees and rocks would not figure for them among the things they notice, register and have names for. The world would present itself quite differently to these creatures; it would be structured and organized for them in ways entirely alien to us. It would be silly − parochial, hubristic, invidious − for us to suppose that these creatures have got the world wrong, and that only the perspective of we (modern) human beings offers a true mirror of reality. No less silly, as Friedrich Nietzsche observed, than for a gnat to imagine that the gnat's-eye view of the world is privileged, the view that uniquely corresponds to reality (Nietzsche 1979: 79).

What is emerging is that none of the terms we employ in everyday descriptions of the world has a claim to refer to the world as it is 'in itself' or 'as such' − to a world that, as Buddhists put it, is 'not conditioned' by human perception and purpose. It is impossible, as William James rightly remarked, to 'weed out the human factor' from such descriptions (James 1977: 455). And it is impossible to imagine how the world might present itself to a creature who was entirely without interests and perspectives − one who was an absolutely pure and detached spectator of the passing scene. This is impossible, not because our powers of imagination are stunted, but because it makes no sense to suppose that a world would be present at all to such a creature. Things stand out for us and light up for us − and for any other creatures − only through the significance they have within a web of life, a life that is charged with desires, goals and values. A world, one might say, is a theatre of significance. For a world − a structured whole of things − to be anything for us it must be experienced, and experience is inseparable from a web of life, a network of meanings.

So any world that can be described is not unconditioned reality, not the way things are 'as such'. This unconditioned reality − this way of things − must be nameless, ineffable, mysterious. At any rate, this is a conclusion we should accept once we have addressed and rejected a couple of alternative proposals, to which I briefly turn.

THE SCIENTIFIC IMAGE

Everyday terms of ordinary English – 'flute', 'tree', 'bird', 'temple' – do not, we've seen, describe the way of things, the way they are independent of interest-driven perspectives. But perhaps we're looking in the wrong place, at the wrong sort of vocabulary. Perhaps there's another kind of language that does have a legitimate claim to capture reality 'as such', one that has shaken off the constraints imposed by all-too-human interests and perspectives.

If I were a biologist, I might return from my walk through the garden and describe the plants and creatures I encountered in a specialist vocabulary. I would speak – not of trees and birds – but of cells, neurones, DNA processes and so on. And if I was familiar with state-of-the-art theoretical physics, I might try to translate this vocabulary into one referring to sub-atomic particles, quantum events or whatever. I might then insist that this vocabulary of physics, unlike that of everyday experience, provides a uniquely and objectively true description of the way of things.

But I would be deluding myself, and it is a conceit to imagine that the language of science is a privileged one that provides an accurate mirror of nature. The conceit is not that of science itself. There is no need to reject the biochemist's description of a tree in terms of cellular structure and biochemical processes – no more than there is to reject everyday descriptions of the tree that employ words like 'leaf', 'trunk' and 'lichen'. It is not science, but what is sometimes called *scientism*, that is guilty of conceit. Scientism is an attitude towards science, to the effect that science – and science alone – can furnish an objective, fundamental account of reality in itself. The way of things, according to this conceit, is the way that physics presents it as being.

Philosophers sometimes speak of 'the scientific image' of the world. The phrase is an apt one, for it suggests, rightly, that science is just that – one image, among many possible ones, of how things are. It is an image that it is especially useful to employ for certain purposes – notably those of predicting events and controlling them. Probing what things are made of – molecules, DNA ribbons, or whatever – and the statistical regularities they obey is very helpful in finding out what they are likely to do and how we may influence what they will do. Without such enquiries, cars and bridges could not be built. Technology is more than applied science; it is the ground on which the edifice of science is erected.

That scientism is a conceit becomes apparent when we further reflect on the immense amount of luck that was needed for science ever to have developed and then become entrenched in the manner it has. History might easily have gone differently, and if it had human beings would have developed schemes of understanding and explanation quite different from those of the natural sciences. The confident assertion that, unlike the sciences, these other schemes of understanding would not have mirrored reality, is no more warranted than the conviction of Nietzsche's gnats that their perspective alone gets it all right.

We should reflect, too, on how parasitic upon our ordinary experience of the world the scientific image is. It's only because experience presents us with a world of trees, birds and other inhabitants of nature that scientists have anything in front of them to get to work on, to dissect, analyse and hypothesize about. Had the world presented itself to us very differently – as it presumably does to gnats – there is no reason to think that enquiry into this world would yield anything remotely like the natural sciences as we know them.

Reflect, too, that our interests and aims might have been very different from what they now are. Suppose, say, we had lived in a land of milk and honey, where everything we needed for survival, comfort and pleasure was readily supplied, without planning or effort on our part. Predicting and controlling events would then have mattered to us much less. These practices are imperative only in a world of shortage, uncertainty and peril. Lotus-eating, aesthetic appreciation of nature might have mattered much more to the men and women we are imagining than the achievement of practical mastery of nature. In the unlikely event that science, in a form that we could recognize as science, had developed in such a culture, it would have been a pastime of marginal interest. It would have been of no more moment and importance for these people than literary criticism, for example, is for most of us today in our own more pragmatic culture. Certainly it would have been nothing that people would have regarded as delineating the fundamental contours of reality.

My lotus-eating aesthetes would be unwilling, I'm confident, to subordinate their everyday, sensory experience of the world – a world of colours, smells, tastes – to a scientific account of the world that avoids all mention of these sensory items. And, in this respect, we should be on the side of the lotus-eaters. It is an implication of privileging the scientific image of the world that what is sometimes called our 'manifest' image of it is relegated to the realm of illusion. Leaves and bird-calls manifest themselves to us as green or brown, loud or soft. But colours and sounds do not feature in the scientific image – not if by colours and sounds we have in mind, as of course we generally do, the simple sensory features that we see or hear. The scientist might define green and loud in terms of emissions of light-waves or sound-waves that impinge on eye or ear. But that's not what you or I mean by colours and sounds, not what is presented to our experience.

In the scientific image, the vibrant world of colours, sounds and tastes is a screen, a veil, between us and the real – colourless, soundless, tasteless – universe of particles and quantum processes. And, of course, in that image the qualities of beauty, elegance, wonder and meaning with which the manifest world is also replete – these, too, belong only in the realm of illusion, as 'subjective' effects, as happenings 'in the mind' that, pathetically, we suppose to belong to the world itself. There is an irony in those many television science programmes where a wide-eyed, gobsmacked presenter invites us to gaze at or listen to such 'wonders of nature' as the aurora borealis or the singing of whales. For, on the physicist's conception of the world assumed in such programmes to be true, the colours and sounds that we, like the presenter, experience do not belong in the world at all. We are being invited to wonder at what isn't there.

This relegation of the manifest and the ordinary is something we should resist. Indeed, none of us seriously accepts, when we are engaged in the thick of life, the thought that the world as ordinarily experienced is a façade beyond which lurks the real thing, the universe of the physicist. More likely, we'll think of that universe, along with Goethe, as a 'grey, corpse-like spectre' (Goethe 2011: §XI).

The scientific image, however, is not the only rival to a doctrine of mystery. I want now to turn to a fashionable view that rejects mystery and the scientific image alike.

THE WORLD AS FICTION

'But a garden, you see, is actually a text – something you need to "read" as you stroll through it.' Remarks like this, not only about gardens, but about towns, human history, clothing and food, natural environments – about everything, in effect – were very popular not so long ago in the corridors of French and American universities crowded with disciples of the movement known as postmodernism. The metaphor of the world as a text was, perhaps, the essential expression of the philosophical wing of this movement. But how is the metaphor to be unpacked?

First, it conveys the sensible thought that to recognize walls as walls, flutes as flutes, and so on, is to understand their significance. Just as the lines in a poem are understood through the contribution they make to the text as a whole, so items like walls are understood in terms of their relationship to a larger whole – as separating a lawn from a terrace in a garden, for example. And just as words are understood against a background of human practices which they help us to conduct, so walls, and flutes, are understood to be what they are only in the light of the practices, the web of life, in which they have significance. In part, therefore, the postmodernist metaphor is giving expression to the point I made earlier – that things figure for us only as items in networks of meaning.

The world as text, however, has a much more radical sense for many postmodernist writers. A text is a human creation or construct, the product of a human project. To think of the world as text is therefore to regard it as a construct or projection – a fiction, in effect. Beyond the world as it is described and experienced in terms of humanly constructed concepts there is nothing. No sense can therefore be given to the idea of a reality 'beyond the human', beyond the fictional products of human intelligence and purpose. There is, as a celebrated postmodernist slogan has it, nothing outside of the text (Derrida 1988: 144).

One implication of this radical claim can be welcomed: its rejection of scientism. If there is nothing beyond the text, then the world we experience is not a veil between us and a truer universe described, on the scientistic view, by the physical sciences. The scientist's universe, for the postmodernist, is just one more text – one more story, useful for certain purposes, for people to tell. It can have no more validity – no more correspondence to anything outside the text – than the stories told by religion and myth.

It is not only scientism, however, that is an intended target of the postmodernist polemic. So is a doctrine of mystery of the type I proposed a few pages back. According to this doctrine, any world that can be described is an all-too-human, perspectival one – a text, if you like – that does not exist independently of human interests and practices. But this does not mean that there is no realm of being 'beyond the human'. What it does mean is that such a realm – the way of things – would be ineffable, mysterious. For the postmodernist, by contrast, there is nothing at all 'beyond the human', effable or ineffable. If the so-called real world is simply text, then nothing at all besides human practice and intelligence is responsible for there being such a world.

This is not, I want to say, a thought with which it is possible to live. People may mouth postmodernist slogans to the effect that there is nothing beyond the text, but they cannot seriously subscribe to these slogans. This is not because the idea of the world as nothing but a human construct is logically absurd. Accepting it is impossible, rather, because we cannot seriously live with the thought that there is no ground for beliefs, purposes and values. We cannot, in honesty, suppose that these are answerable to nothing at all besides the human practices and decisions that have produced them. Postmodernist rhetoric of being faithful to nothing besides our own conventions, decisions and choices is simply that – rhetoric. It may sound good in the seminar room, the columns of a Parisian literary journal, or over a drink in a bar, but it is not something that people can take seriously when they are in the stream of life, when they are actually having to form beliefs, make important decisions, and teach their children what to honour and what to despise.

I can read and enjoy a novel without demanding that the beliefs and commitments of its characters be grounded in anything. But I cannot take the same attitude towards my own beliefs and commitments, nor towards those of people who matter to me. I cannot but consider these commitments to be answerable to something, to have a measure beyond themselves, to be subject to an authority besides my own dedication to them. A commitment – to raising a family, say, or writing a work of philosophy, or training to be a nurse – could not survive the recognition that it has no warrant beyond it being one that I happened to have made. If I came to see it in that way, it would cease to be a commitment; it would lose any hold on me.

Nor can I regard my experience of the world around me – its creatures, its landscapes, its beauties – as having no source other than human invention. I cannot but take my experience seriously, as being authentic, and therefore as having a ground or source that justifies me in respecting and cultivating this experience. Otherwise I could not move about and act in this world, for I could place no weight or significance on anything that I or other people see, hear or do. To reduce the world to a text means that the world would at best, as Schopenhauer put it, pass me by like an empty dream (Schopenhauer 1969: 99). At worst, it is an inducement to insanity or suicide.

So we cannot but think of experience, beliefs, values and commitments as having a source or measure 'beyond the human'. At the same time, though, we should not rescind the claim that any world we can describe and conceptualize – any discursable world, that is – is a human world, one encountered and structured only in relation to purposes and practices. Let's reflect for a moment on the seeming tension between these two claims.

THE WORLD AS GIFT

The issue is a delicate one. How might we hang on to the thought that the world we experience is dependent on human perspective and interest without downgrading or impugning this world – without turning it into something superficial or shadowy? How might we think about the mystery of being – the ineffable way of things – if we are not to lose confidence in everyday experience and in the possibility of authenticating a sense of what matters and what is good? How do we avoid treating what we experience as a fiction, as a veil between us and the truly real?

To help with this issue, we need to accept and absorb three related thoughts. First, we should try to dispel an image people sometimes have of the mysterious as belonging to a foreign land, a distant or 'transcendent' realm that is without connection to the everyday world of experience. Instead, we should think of the ineffable way of things as a source, a well-spring of the world of experience. If we don't think of it like this, it is hard to see how acknowledging the existence of mystery could help to provide confidence in everyday experience and any guidance on how our lives should be led. Remember that it was precisely the need for our beliefs, perceptions, commitments and values to be answerable to something – to have a measure – that compelled acknowledgement of a realm of mystery, a realm 'beyond the human'.

Second, we should borrow a metaphor that's employed in several religious traditions – that of the world as a gift. Our experience of the world is an authentic way in which things have become present to and for us; not a distorting screen between us and reality, not some illusion to which we have fallen victim. The world of experience is, to recall the Zen master Dōgen's words, 'something ineffable coming like this' – like, that is, the trees, the birds, the colours and sounds that were vividly presented to me on that evening in the garden. The ineffable, the way of things, is a constant giving to which we are, or should be, receptive.

Third, as those last words suggest, we should think of the ineffable way of things as inseparable from the world of experience that it gives. It is not, for example, a creator god, a being who is splendidly independent of the world that he created. To think of the source of the world in such theistic terms – as a special being, person and intelligence – is to be guilty of applying all-too-human concepts to what is beyond conceptualization and description. It is worth, in this connection, taking seriously, as does Martin Heidegger, such metaphors as 'source' and 'well-spring' (Heidegger 1966: 55, 76, 88). Just as the source or spring of a stream is not separate from the water that flows from it, so the mysterious source of the world is inseparable from the world of experience that flows from this source. The language here is, of course, irremediably figurative, for there can be no literal description of what is ineffable. So we grope for metaphors and analogies – source, stream, spring and so on – that give an intimation at least of the contours of mystery.

It is the crucial, though delicate and difficult, thought of the inseparability of mystery and world that is expressed in the texts of several religious traditions, for example Daoist and Buddhist. The way, the *dao*, is 'not separated from' but 'fills the entire world', as one Chinese text, the *Nei-yeh*, puts it (Roth 1999: 49). That which 'makes beings beings' – the *dao* – is, the Daoist master Zhuangzi explains, 'not separated from them by any border' (Zhuangzi 2009: Ch. 22). In a similar vein, as D.T. Suzuki explains, the texts of Mahayana Buddhism teach us that the 'unconditioned', which is the ineffable 'font and source' of the world of experience, does not exist independently of this world of 'forms' and objects that are 'accessible to discursive thought' (in Mitchell 1998: 43). In the writings of both traditions, the aim is to dispel the image of a super-being that created the world, and to encourage, instead, the idea of the world as a gift that – like the water we drink from a stream – is received by us as flowing from a source. The world as an integrated whole of experience is given to us, but not by any agent that could be described as a giver.

These last remarks – and, indeed, my defence of mystery itself – have, unsurprisingly, drawn us into the domain of religious discourse. In the next chapter, I'll begin by offering some remarks on religion and its relationship to mystery.

REFERENCES

Conze, E. (tr.) 1990, *The Large Sūtra on Perfect Wisdom*, Delhi: Banarsidass.

Cooper, D.E. 2002, *The Measure of Things: Humanism, Humility and Mystery*, Oxford: Oxford University Press.

Derrida, J. 1988, *Limited Inc.*, Evanston, IL: Northwestern University Press

Dōgen. 1996, *Shobogenzo*, Vol ii, London: Windbell.

Goethe, J.W. 2011, *Wahrheit und Dichtung*, Fischer Klassik, Kindle ed.

Heidegger, M. 1966, *Discourse on Thinking*, New York: Harper & Row.

James, W. 1977, *Pragmatism and Humanism*, in *The Writings of William James*, Chicago: University of Chicago Press.

Laozi. 2003, *The Daodejing of Laozi*, Indianapolis, IN: Hackett.

Mitchell, D. (ed.) 1998, *Masao Abe: A Zen Life of Dialogue*, Boston: Tuttle.

Nietzsche, F. 1979, *Philosophy and Truth: Selections from Nietzsche's Notebooks of the Early 1870s*, Atlantic Highlands, NJ: Humanities.

Roth, H. 1999, *Original Tao: Inward Training (Nei-yeh) and the Foundation of Taoist Mysticism*, New York: Columbia University Press.

Schopenhauer, A. 1969, *The World as Will and Representation*, Vol i, New York: Dover.

Zhuangzi. 2009, *Zhuangzi: The Essential Writings*, Indianapolis, IN: Hackett.

3

RELIGION, NATURE AND MYSTERY

RELIGION, FAITH, MYSTERY

For some readers, the idea of mystery easily slides into that of mysticism. And this is a term prone to evoke the style of religiosity conveyed by images of the ecstatic saints of medieval Sufism or Counter-Reformation Catholicism.

I have myself been citing texts, including Buddhist ones, that are often described as 'religious'. So, is the philosophy of mystery I am defending a religious one? There is a reason that is sometimes given for saying 'No'. In the West and the Middle East, the concept of religion is closely tied to that of God, to the notion of an omnipotent being that created the universe. The religions with the largest followings in those regions are theistic ones – the Abrahamic religions of Christianity, Judaism and Islam – so it is unsurprising that religion and theism have become coupled in people's understanding. To ears that are attuned to the description of religiousness as belief in God, the expression 'atheistic religion', sometimes used to refer to Buddhism, Jainism and Daoism, sounds like a contradiction in terms.

At the end of the day, perhaps it does not matter so very much whether the label 'religious' is applied to the kind of sensibility – an openness to mystery – that I am defending and proposing ways to cultivate. But the reason just cited for witholding the label is one that we should resist. This is not simply because otherwise we are forced to deny the title of religion, not only to such dispensations as Buddhism, Jainism and Daoism, but to the many native spiritual traditions that have flourished in, for example, the Americas and Australia. Nor is the main objection that, in the Abrahamic religions themselves, there have also been 'mystical' tendencies in which it is not the person of God, but something more recessive, more resistant to description – the Godhead, Ein sof ('the unlimited') – that is the ultimate ground of the universe. These tendencies, after all, were generally condemned, and often pronounced blasphemous, by defenders of the orthodox doctrines challenged by the mystics. Many Sufi adepts, for instance, were put to death.

The more important objection to tying religion and theism closely together is that doing so exaggerates the role of doctrinal belief within religions. Primacy is in effect being given to believing that certain propositions are true, at the expense of the role played in religion by practices, rituals and emotions. A person should not be described as religious simply because he or she ticks as 'True' propositions like 'God exists' or 'The world was created by God'. It is perfectly possible – indeed very common these days – for someone to subscribe to such propositions but for these beliefs to play no significant part in the person's life. This life should not be regarded as a religious one.

The point can be made in terms of the idea of faith. A religious person is one whose life is informed and shaped, at least in part, by a religious sense. Essential to this sense is faith or confidence. But faith is not simply, or centrally, a matter of assent to certain propositions or doctrines. If, as Tolstoy saw it, faith 'gives the possibility of living' – is a 'force whereby we live' – it cannot consist solely in doctrinal assent (in James

1923: 184). Rather, it is a kind of confidence in the way of life one is following, a confidence that this is in harmony with the larger way of things, and a way that leads to fulfilment. It may, as with Buddhists, derive from a confidence or faith in a particular human being, like Gautama, as a man whose beauty, grace and comportment manifest an understanding of things and of how to live. Or it may be a confidence that is both expressed in and deepened by the performance of rituals whose dignity and beauty owe – or so the adept feels – to their consonance with truth, to their being founded on and faithful to insight into the way of things.

Religiousness, wrote Ludwig Wittgenstein, is to be perceived above all as 'really a way of living, of assessing life' in keeping with a certain confidence – a feeling perhaps of being *safe* in this way of living (Wittgenstein 1980: 64). If this is right, then there is no objection to regarding as religious a life led in mindfulness of the mystery of things. To live well, said Black Elk, the famous Lakotan Sioux holy man, is to do so 'in a manner suited to the way the Sacred Power of the world lives and moves'. It is to do so with 'a view of the world as a place of sacred mystery', the gift of Wakan Tanka, 'the great spirit' whom 'not even the gods can understand', let alone we mere humans (Neihardt 2014: 129). What Black Elk describes here is surely a religious life, one led in the confidence that it answers well to a mysterious way of things.

Nothing momentous, perhaps, finally turns on whether the term 'religious' is applied to a life informed by a sense of mystery, and those who find it impossible to shake off the association of the term with belief in God as a person may stick with expressions like 'spiritual' or 'sacred'. I'm comfortable, personally, with using the term and will continue to do so where it seems appropriate. The more urgent matter, however, is to reflect on the idea of a sense of mystery and the cultivation of this sense.

'NOTHING SPECIAL'

I've urged that the place of beliefs in religious practices and attitudes – of holding certain propositions to be true – should not be exaggerated. A similar point needs to be made with respect to a view of the world that recognizes mystery. I have referred, it's true, to a doctrine of mystery – and have tried, in the preceding chapter, to persuade you of its truth. But it would be wrong to equate appreciation of the mystery of things with accepting as true philosophical remarks like those I made in defence of mystery. It is not difficult to imagine a student who is unable to find anything wrong with those remarks and happy to regurgitate them in an exam answer. But easy to imagine, as well, that this student is not someone in whom the idea of mystery has, in William James' phrase, grown 'hot and alive' (James 1923: 197). The student respectfully nods in agreement with the lecturer's defence of mystery, but then passes on – his or her life barely affected, and certainly not infused, by it. In the words of the Buddha, this belief in a doctrine has not been 'deeply cultivated' or 'well-established', since a 'right view', if it is genuinely embraced, must engage with practice and feeling (Bodhi 2005: 281ff).

It is, then, a sense of mystery – not mere assent to a doctrine – that needs to be cultivated; otherwise this assent is hollow. For some people, the strategy for cultivation of a sense of mystery may be to seek out 'mystical experiences' – direct and dramatic encounters with the ineffable, visions of a realm beyond the understanding, or trance-like insights afforded by motionless, virtuoso contemplation. But this is not, I think, where the focus should be, and the strategy is one that raises several concerns.

To begin with, special mystical experiences, visions and virtuoso feats of meditation are not for everyone. I don't want dogmatically to deny that such things occur or to insist that what they seem to deliver is illusion. But it is clear that if most of us are to enjoy and develop a sense of mystery, it must be along a path that is not reserved for a handful of visionaries and adepts.

Second, these special experiences – precisely because they are special – are hived off, or disjoined, from the flow of everyday life. They are staccato moments that are not integrated with a person's general experience of the world. They do not – to continue the musical analogy – lend a tone to a person's life; rather, they are single, separated percussive notes. If a sense of mystery is to provide a measure for a person's beliefs, practices and commitments, it needs to be something that may pervade the person's life – lending it an enduring tone or complexion.

A related and perhaps paramount concern is that equating a sense of mystery with the deliverances of mystical states, visions or meditative trances exemplifies and encourages a familiar, but false, opposition. This is the opposition between, on the one hand, religious or spiritual experience and, on the other, ordinary perceptual or sensory experience. It is only recently that theologians have questioned the unfortunate but entrenched tendency in the principal Western religions to regard sensory experience as at best irrelevant to religious understanding, and at worst an obstacle (see Wynn 2013). Little attention has been paid to the possibility that it is in and through sensory perception of the empirical world that spiritual understanding may be at once exercised and deepened.

My focus, therefore, will be upon cultivation of a sense of mystery through experiences of the world that are not disjoined from everyday life. They are not experiences that are obtained only in separation from the stream of ordinary life. To recall the expression of which followers of Zen are fond, these experiences and engagements are 'nothing special'. It is, more generally, in the traditions of Asia, unlike those of the West, that the contrast between spiritual and everyday experience has been rejected, or at any rate softened.

What shows through in many of the practices and texts of Buddhism, Daoism, Jainism and Shinto is the conviction that the vehicle of a sense of mystery – of the way of things – is ordinary life itself when this is conducted mindfully and in an appropriate style. If most of my allusions to the literatures and cultures of mystery are to non-Western traditions, that is the reason.

SENSES OF MYSTERY

I have referred on many occasions to a sense of mystery, but the title of this book is *Senses of Mystery*. Why the plural? It's partly because, lurking in the title, is a pun. 'Senses' can refer not just to intimations or feelings but to the perceptual senses of sight, touch, hearing and so on. As we've just seen, it is an important theme in the book that it is through ordinary sensory experience that attunement to mystery is possible. The senses, one might say, can work to inspire a sense of mystery.

The main reason, however, for the plural in the title is that it is possible and helpful to distinguish different aspects or modes of mystery. It is not exactly that there are several separate mysteries on which to reflect. The ineffable way of things is not anything we can describe and articulate so as to then divide it up into discrete compartments. But there are different faces or aspects of mystery that offer themselves to attention and reflection.

An analogy – only a partial one, to be sure – might help. People may be impressed by a vague, but powerful, sense of what they discern as the wonder – the mystery, if you will – of music. But it is then towards rather different aspects of music that they may direct their wonder. It may be a particular piece of music that inspires and invites their reflections. How, they might ask, is it possible that a piece of such sublimity could ever have been created? Or it may be a more general phenomenon that is the focus of wonder – the emergence of music as a human capacity. How do we explain how human beings ever came to produce certain organized sounds and experience these as music? Or the wonder may be directed at the more metaphysically charged question of the very source of music. Could those Greek and medieval thinkers have been right, people might ask, to postulate an inaudible and abstract 'music of the spheres' – a *musica universalis* – from which the music that we sing, play and dance to is somehow descended?

Somewhat analogously, an initially vague sense of the mystery of things might crystallize in different ways. Perhaps it is the world's being the particular way it is, and not some other way, that incites a feeling of mystery and becomes the object of reflection. Must it not remain a mystery why our experience of the world is what it is and not entirely different? Or it may be something more general that becomes the focus of reflection – the emergence of any world at all for us to experience. What possible explanation could there be for the emergence of experience as such – as distinct from experience of this or that world in particular? Or, finally, the sense of mystery may attach to the very source of experience and worldhood. Were the compilers of the *Daodejing* not right to hold that this source – the *dao* – is nameless, ineffable?

We might call these aspects of mystery those of *world*, *emergence* and *source*. It's worth noting that, in some theological systems, these mysteries can be prised apart. Some writers have argued, for example, that while it is mysterious why God created the world at all, there is no mystery as to its source – namely, God – nor as to why it's the particular way it is. It's because it is perfect that way. Any other world, argued Leibniz, would not have been 'the best of all possible worlds', and not one, therefore, that God – being perfect – would have created (Leibniz 1952: I.8).

But if you think back on the case for mystery that I put forward in Chapter 2, you'll see that, in my view, the three faces of mystery are faces of something indivisible, ones that can't be torn or prised apart. The source of worldhood and experience is not an effable God; it is ineffable, and hence the emergence from this source of a world of experience is a mystery. And so is the particular configuration of experience we call our world, the actual world. There cannot, we saw, be an objective account of the world – independent of the practices and purposes of creatures like ourselves – in terms of which to explain why experience is as it is. But nor, we also saw, could anyone seriously think that there is nothing 'beyond the human' – nothing at all to which our experience, beliefs and commitments are answerable.

Despite remaining linked to one another, it is possible and helpful, I said, to distinguish the three faces of mystery. A main reason why it is helpful to do so is that the experiences and intimations that I'll describe – all of which serve to cultivate a sense of mystery – vary as to the aspect of mystery onto which, as it were, they latch. Some may foster, in the first instance, a sense of the mystery of the world's being as it is; others, a sense of the mystery of emergence of any world at all; yet others, a sense of the mystery of the source of everything. Together they combine to cultivate a sense of the mystery of the way of things. This will become clearer once I have introduced the modes of experience that will occupy us in the chapters ahead.

NATURE AND CULTURE

The book began with an early evening walk through a Sri Lankan garden – not through a Toronto shopping mall, a Sydney art gallery, or a London church. Why? Because the various elements of my walk through the garden – the act of walking in a natural (if humanly modified) environment, the appreciation of a place as a garden, the presence of birds and animals, the music heard in a natural setting, the feel of old buildings taken over by moss and lichen – are good indications of the kinds of experience and engagement on which I want to focus.

These are kinds of experience and engagement that, when mindfully attended to, attune to mystery. What connects them is, of course, *nature*. They involve perceptions of, or intercourse with, natural beings and phenomena in places where natural processes like growth and decay are palpably at work.

None of the component experiences of my walk consists, however, in detached spectatorship of 'wilderness' – of Nature, with the big 'N' of which the Romantics were fond, untouched by human hands and starkly 'Other' than the realm of culture. I was walking through a garden – not gazing towards a distant range of inaccessible mountains or looking down, as from an aeroplane, onto a vast, uninhabited tundra. A garden is a 'human landscape', not simply in the obvious sense of being physically shaped by human beings, but also in virtue of its meaning in the lives of the men and women who made it, care for it and enjoy it. That is why the garden is a good metaphor for the natural world considered in its relationship with human life, with culture. And it is why it provides an especially apt setting for experiences, like listening to music outdoors, that result from an interplay between human practice and receptivity to natural environments.

But why do I focus on these 'hybrid' experiences, where culture and nature meet, rather than upon ones gained in an urban art gallery or church, or upon those yielded by looking at wilderness? Well, we are in search of symbols or ciphers, seeking to identify experiences and encounters that are suited to bring us to a sense of mystery. We are looking for experiences of things, processes or phenomena that help to make salient the truth of mystery. Now, the truth of mystery, I argued, is this: any world we can articulate is a human world, shaped by our practices and purposes, not reality 'as such'. Yet we cannot but believe that there is a 'beyond the human' that is responsible for the arising of this world – something that, since it does not belong in the human world, must be ineffable, mysterious.

Experiences that are good for conveying – for giving us a feel for – this truth need to have two dimensions. On the one hand, they must remind us that our perception of the world is a human perspective, not a confrontation with reality 'as such'. At the same time, however, they must foster a sense of this world as being mysteriously 'given' by what is 'beyond the human'. The city and the wilderness fail, for opposed reasons, to perform these twin tasks. The city fails because it presents us with the all-too-human, with a world of artefact, of culture without nature. Wilderness fails because it presents us with what is all-too-inhuman, a world of nature devoid of cultural imprint. The city does nothing to encourage a sense of human practice owing to anything beyond itself. The city is experienced as the product of invention and technology, an emphatically and strikingly human achievement. Wilderness, conversely, does nothing to promote a sense of the world as owing anything at all to human perspectives. It is encountered as being just there, as 'objective', as already formed independently of the interests and purposes of creatures like ourselves. It is simply 'Other'.

It is an illusion, if I'm right, to think of the city as the product solely of human practice, and a complementary illusion to think of wilderness as independent of human perspective. But that's not to the present point. We are, to recall, in the business of searching for symbols, ciphers, metaphors of mystery. These won't be found among experiences – of the city or of wilderness – that, for contrasting reasons, mask the double-barrelled truth of mystery: the dependence of the world on human perspective, and the mysterious 'gift' of this world from an ineffable source of things.

This maybe sounds more dogmatic than I intend. I certainly don't want to deny that a sense of mystery might, on certain occasions, be prompted by experiences in an art gallery or church, or by emotions felt when looking at a vast, virgin wilderness. Ways to a sense of mystery are not ones that can be fixed, and it would be wrong to pre-empt a whole range of possible ways. Followers of Zen, after all, record intimations of mystery being elicited by boiling rice, sweeping floors and chopping firewood.

But we are talking of aptness, and I hope the following chapters will confirm my judgement that the kinds of experiences I describe – of 'hybrids' of nature and culture – are especially apt to intimate the truth of mystery. There are, to be sure, many more kinds of experience of 'hybrids' than those, like gardening and walking, that I will be discussing. My selection is, inevitably, coloured by my background, enthusiasms and sensibilities. For example, I do a reasonable amount of walking in the countryside, but I have never been kayaking or cross-country skiing. I spend a lot of time in the garden and in the company of blackbirds and robins, but I have never been a forester or been close to the eagles and buzzards that soar above the forest. I am unable to comment on the potential of activities with which I have no familiarity for attuning men and women to the mystery of things. In today's vernacular, the experiences on which I focus are ones that 'work for me'. That they work for me does not, I think, mean that I'm eccentric in this respect. But nor, of course, do I want to deny that it is different engagements with nature that work for other people. What follows, then, is an exploration of ways to a sense of mystery that are personal but not, I hope, idiosyncratic.

REFERENCES

Bodhi, Bhikkhu (ed.) 2005, *In the Buddha's Words: An Anthology of Discourses from the Pāli Canon*, Boston: Wisdom Publications.

James, W. 1923, *The Varieties of Religious Experience*, New York: Longmans, Green & Co.

Leibniz, G.W. 1952, *Theodicy*, New Haven, CT: Yale University Press.

Neihardt, J.G. (ed.) 2014, *Black Elk Speaks: The Complete Edition*, Lincoln, NB: University of Nebraska Press.

Wittgenstein, L. 1980, *Culture and Value*, Oxford: Blackwell.

Wynn, M.R. 2013, *Renewing the Senses: A Study of the Philosophy and Theology of the Spiritual Life*, Oxford: Oxford University Press.

4

ANIMALS

ANIMAL WORLDS

Where to begin? The natural, though not inevitable, place to start is with the first of the aspects or modes of mystery that I distinguished a few pages back. This is what I called the mystery of the world – the mystery of the world's being as it is, of things figuring for us as they do. My aim is not to repeat or develop the argument for thinking that there is indeed mystery here, but to identify ways of experiencing and engaging with the natural world that promote a sense of, a feel for, this mystery.

My stroll through the garden brought me into proximity with animals – with birds, frogs, fish and other creatures whose identity I could only guess at from the noises they made. Attending in certain ways to animals, I propose, is apt to promote a sense of the world's mystery. What ways are these? Not, certainly, the kind of attention paid by scientists who attend exclusively to the biology of animals – their glands, muscles, nervous systems or DNA composition. Nor the kind paid by experimental psychologists who are focused upon the overt behaviour of animals without any concern with what it might be like to be an animal – with what most of us, unlike some of these psychologists, would be happy to call animal consciousness. The attention to, or experience of, animals that is relevant for us is a kind that recognizes animals as purposive agents, creatures with perspectives on the world, as subjects and not mere things. It is with animals as beings that have and lead lives that we will be concerned.

The sorts of experiences of, or with, animals that are relevant are – with some important qualifications – those afforded to animal trainers, hunters, and people who live with pets or companion animals. The qualifications, though, are essential. The trainers I have in mind are not those who beat animals – performing bears, circus elephants and the rest – into blind and terrified submission. They are those who recognize that, in order to guarantee intelligent cooperation on the part of a dog, horse or hawk, it is essential to understand and respect the needs, feelings and intelligence of the animal. By 'hunters', I do not mean the men who, between mouthfuls of lobster and champagne, enjoy massacring pheasants or wild boars on weekend country shoots. I mean men in traditional societies that depended upon hunting for food and clothing. These were men who often honoured the bears or wolves that they perceived as giving up their lives to them, and who certainly knew how essential to the success of the hunt was empathetic understanding of their quarry. And the pet owners I am thinking of are not the ones who disguise from themselves the animality of their companion animals, but those who try to understand, appreciate and heed what it is like to be a dog or a cat that has been inducted into a human family.

To be acquainted with and to appreciate the lives of animals, however, it is not necessary to be a trainer, hunter or pet owner. Just being watchful in the garden is sufficient for becoming familiar with the lives of the frog that keeps appearing on the patio, the pair of swallows that constantly fly in and out of an old hut, and the bees that enjoy the buddleia. These lives, too, need to be understood if the gardener is to encourage and protect these creatures. Nor does it have to be gardens, as we usually picture them, in which this empathy with animals is exercised. It was in a protected woodland that the Buddha and an elephant enjoyed a mutual understanding − their minds 'united' − of a need to escape from the jostle of the crowd or herd (Ireland 1990: Ch. 4.5).

One reason to focus on the experience of animals gained by people who engage with them in the ways mentioned is that it exposes the absurdity of the question − asked, with apparent seriousness, by some psychologists and philosophers − of whether animals are mere machines, lacking in any mental life. Such questions can be asked only by someone who is determined to regard the movements of animals as 'data' from which to infer − or refuse to infer − the existence of something 'inner' going on. But this is a very strange attitude. Think of the reaction if this person were to regard his wife and children in the same manner. Someone who lives with a dog does not treat its sounds and movements as *evidence* − reliable or otherwise − of the animal's feelings and wants. He or she can see or hear in these movements or sounds the fear, anticipation or contentment of the dog. Nor, when I am in my garden at home, can I seriously doubt that the swallows are anxious at the proximity of a magpie or that the frog I hold in my hand wants to be put back in the little hole from which it emerged and where it feels safe.

Wiser than worrying about the existence of animal 'consciousness' and 'minds' − on what 'inner' events are going on in the creature − is to emphasize that, like us, animals have worlds and environments. By this, I don't mean simply that a hedgehog, for example, is somewhere rather than nowhere, that its life takes place in a certain geographical area. We should hear the term 'environment' here more in the sense it has when we speak, for instance, of a home, school or working environment. An environment, in this sense, is not a spatially defined area, but a sphere of significance, a place or context that people understand and engage with. It is an ambience in which things are meaningful, in which people move easily and act with purpose. The hedgehog, too, has an environment in this sense: things matter to it and figure for it in various ways – as food, shelter, predator, mate and so on. It understands this environment, is at home there, and knows its way about it, not just in the thin sense of not getting lost, but of moving through it with ease in pursuit of its aims, to meet the needs of itself and its family.

A distressing way in which it becomes apparent that animals typically have environments in the sense explained is to observe the result of denying them the environments they know. To watch a listless, dull-eyed wolf in a zoo or a bored yet anxious monkey in a laboratory cage is to realize how the flourishing lives of more fortunate animals are defined by the environments suited to them. It is not the geographical dislocation – across the sea to a foreign zoo, say – that is crucial per se, but the removal of the animal from a context, a theatre of significance, in which it is at home. (Compare the effect of placing a man or a woman in a prison cell where the scope for meaningful activity is severely circumscribed.) The Book of Zhuangzi is replete with examples of how – often cruelly, and always stupidly – birds, horses and other creatures are forced by human beings into alien environments where things no longer figure for the animals in ways they understand and can cope with (Zhuangzi 2009: Chs 6, 9, 19). But some of Zhuangzi's examples are designed to show, not only that animals do indeed have environments and perspectives of their own, but something else – the opacity, to us, of these perspectives.

THE OPACITY OF ANIMALS

Zhuangzi is in no doubt that it is distressing for wild horses to be taken from the prairies where they love to gallop and then branded and corralled. But he is much less sure when it comes to divining the thoughts of butterflies or the emotions of fish. He's right to be less sure, and even the lives of the animals we are most familiar with are sometimes opaque to us. One philosopher nicely compares the relationship between a pet and its owner as being more like a dance – in which each responds spontaneously to the movements and gestures of the other – than to that between people striving to decode what is going on inside one another. But he also notes that the gaze of even the closest of companion animals may sometimes strike its owner as unnervingly alien (James 2009: 43, 131). The point is confirmed by the author of an acclaimed book that records her experiences as an animal trainer. Writing of her own dog, she remarks that it is an 'illusion' to think she could 'penetrate [his] otherness' – that, for example, she could fully share in his understanding of the command 'Sit!' (Hearne 2007: 30).

If our own dogs and cats can be opaque to us, this is all the more true of creatures whose lives and interests are still less like our own and with which we have little familiarity. While I have some grasp of what it is like to be a domestic dog, I have a decreasingly firm grasp of what it is like to be a hyena, a swallow, a bat, a minnow and an ant. Part of the reason for opacity, of course, is that animals – some more than others – are significantly different from ourselves in the sensory apparatus, the organs of perception, through which the world impinges upon them. A dog's remarkable sensitivity to smell means that its experience of the field we walk through together is strikingly different from mine. The orientation and the structure of the eyes of a crow means that its view of the landscape below is importantly unlike the one you would have when hang-gliding. And when we turn to creatures that get around through echolocation or biological sonar, or whose eyes revolve on stems, or that respond to barely measurable vibrations, we are thinking of experiential environments that we can barely imagine.

The larger reason for the opacity of animals, however, is not the difficulty of imagining their sensations, but of understanding how the world figures for creatures whose lives – whose interests, purposes, relationships – are very different from our own. We sometimes say of other human beings – early hunter-gatherers, for example – whose lives are opaque to us that they 'lived in a different world'. This can be said all the more confidently of animals, even of ones very familiar to us. One of Milan Kundera's characters wonders how the command 'Sit!', that she gave to the dog that she knew so well, served to 'give his life meaning' (Kundera 1985: 300).

Here are some of the ways in which the lives and worlds of animals, differing as they do from our own, must be opaque to us. Think, for a start, how much of adult people's experience of the world owes to their having been alive for quite a long time. And then think of the impossibility, therefore, of imagining how the world strikes a creature, like a mayfly, that lives for less than a day. Or consider the extent to which a human being's experience is that of an *individual*. Even the most conformist member of a society that is hide-bound by tradition is a rugged individualist in comparison with most animals. Who knows what the world is like for creatures that live as units in colonies, swarms, hives and flocks?

Despite the individualism of human beings, the world – the meaningful environment – in which you and I move is a context already shaped for us by culture and language. When I walk through a town, the looming shapes around me divide into houses, churches, restaurants and so on – in a way that they cannot do for a mouse or crow. For a creature without culture or language, a town cannot be the same theatre of meaning that it is for me. When those looming shapes are sorted by the mouse or crow, it would be in terms of their potential as shelters or nests.

Culture and language do not just constrain what I can distinguish and categorize, but also the aims, ambitions and many of the emotions it is possible for me to have. An animal cannot want to get promoted or give more to charity, or feel disappointed or resentful when it fails in some long-term ambition. Culture and language also powerfully constrain what practices are possible for people to participate in. Only for creatures like ourselves, who can invent and follow rules, are practices like sport, crime and marriage possible. Even terms like 'eating', that apply to what animals as well as human beings do, have a different sense or tone in the two cases. When I suggest to a colleague that we eat together this evening, I am not proposing simply that we both ingest some edible stuff. Human eating belongs to culture, and even someone who eats alone does so in a manner that reflects the normally social character of eating. He doesn't, like a crocodile, rip a hunk of meat to pieces with his bare teeth, or burrow through a blancmange like a maggot.

To be sure, animals differ greatly among themselves, and the lives of some of them have analogies with the culturally and linguistically shaped ones that we lead. There is not the same degree of strain in describing a dog as jealous, perceptive or disappointed as there is in applying such terms to a mayfly or a frog. The worlds of some animals intersect with our own and with those of other animals, as if in a matrix of Venn diagrams. In a more poetic image, the pioneer of the study of animal environments (*Umwelten*), Jakob von Uexküll, compared the totality of these worlds to a huge 'symphony of meaning' in which 'countless environments', like musical themes and fragments, collide, merge, separate, repeat and modulate (Uexküll 2010: 208).

Maybe it doesn't matter too much whether we speak of there being many worlds, animal and human, or of there being just a single world that is the 'interpenetration' or 'envelopment of

Umwelten in each other' (Merleau-Ponty 2003: 177). Either way, we have the idea of a world as something inseparable from forms of integrated experience – from perspectives – and the related idea of a world as a theatre of significance for beings whose lives are played out within it. Either way, we are discouraged from thinking of the world as a huge spatio-temporal object that could be described independently of any experiential perspective.

Whichever way we speak – whichever metaphors we choose to deploy – it is now time to connect these reflections on animal worlds to the question of the mystery of the world.

ANIMALS, MYSTERY AND WORLD

There are really two questions to ask here. One is how the existence of animal worlds very different from our own supports the conclusion that our world's being as it is is mysterious, inexplicable. The second is how relationships with animals may cultivate a sense of this mystery.

Friedrich Nietzsche was a good classicist. He would have been very familiar with Xenophanes' remark that horses or lions, if they had the requisite skills, would depict the gods as horses or lions, not as men and women. He surely had this in mind when, as we saw earlier, he compared the hubris of human beings in privileging their view of the world with a parallel conceit on the part of a gnat. Underlying Nietzsche's point is his recognition that it is impossible to justify an overall perspective on the ground that it mirrors the objective order of things. This is because a description of this alleged order is bound to be dictated by the very perspective that people – or gnats – are trying to explain and justify. The enterprise is viciously circular.

Someone will respond that the case with gnats, and animals more generally, is quite different from the case with humans. Animals are unable, it'll be said, to rise above a view of the world shaped by their drives and needs, incapable therefore of ascending to an objective view. But I've tried to show that human beings ultimately share the same incapacity. Even the physical sciences fail to describe a world that is independent of human purposes and interests. Jacques Derrida, with Nietzsche in mind, put it like this: '[for us too] everything is in a perspective: the relation to [a being], . . . even the most "objective" . . . is caught in a movement of life . . . it remains an "animal" relation' (Derrida 2008: 160).

Reflection on animal worlds gives force to the truth of perspectivism. If all the creatures we ever encountered shared precisely our view of the world, it would be tempting to suppose that this view is forced upon them and us by the objective structures of reality. But this is not how it is. Animals are living proofs of the existence of many perspectives and of the invidiousness of privileging our own over all the rest. Living proofs, therefore, of the impossibility of explaining or justifying our experience of the world as being a mirror of reality as such.

It is one thing, however, for reflection on animals to confirm that it is a mystery why the world presents itself to us as it does, but another thing for a sense of this mystery to come alive for us. So we need to turn to the second of the questions I raised at the beginning of this section – that of the role of animals in the cultivation of a sense of the world's mystery. In broad outline, the answer to the question is clear enough. If reflection on animals confirms the truth of this mystery, it is *being with* animals that converts recognition of this truth into a sense of the mystery. This is the being with of the figures I described earlier – of men and women who attend to and engage with animals as intelligent, purposive beings. With the caveats I then made, these figures will include many animal trainers, pet owners, and hunters, or simply gardeners mindful of and hospitable to the wildlife that their gardens invite in.

Let's focus on the close human–animal relationship that has been most written about: that of a person to his or her dog. It is a relationship, of course, that comprises many activities on the owner's part – walking the dog, playing with it, stroking its back, feeding it, looking affectionately into eyes that look affectionately back, and so on. There are two things on which those who write best about the human–dog relationship are agreed. First, a person's understanding of the dog is not a matter of *inferring* to its 'inner' states from behavioural data, not some type of scientific conjecture. It comes, as an animal trainer and philosopher puts it, from directly 'listening to the dog's being' (Hearne 2007: 59). Second, they agree that dogs are 'ambiguous'. Thomas Mann remarks, in connection with his short-haired pointer, Bashan, that a dog may be both 'intimate' and 'alien' to a person. At one moment, its nature seems to be 'revealed', at another it seems 'strange' and 'obscure' (Mann 2003: 93).

There are at least three truths that 'listening to a dog's being', and awareness of its 'ambiguity', bring alive for a person. To begin with, no one who seriously engages with the life of a dog can doubt that it is the life of an intelligent, purposive agent that moves through a world that has meaning for it. Bashan's face and movements 'proclaim' his feelings, his sense of having a place in an environment, his intelligent mastery of where, when and what it is appropriate to do. It is because the dog's sphere of meaning intersects with its owner's that there can be intimacy with the animal.

But the second truth that is forced on a person through being with a dog is that its world is, in crucial respects, opaque to even the most loving and empathetic owner. When Bashan meets other dogs, he becomes 'inscrutable', not simply because it is hard to divine his feelings, but because his environment is now governed by 'laws and customs', conceptions and perceptions, that make it a different world from the one Mann himself is moving through and experiencing. A dog may be 'attuned to the human order', but it is attuned as well 'to other orders' (Mann 2003: 84). It is precisely when in close proximity with – real engagement with – a dog or other animal that a person is given a live sense of a creature whose life and practices form a different world from ours.

Vicki Hearne – the philosopher and animal trainer I've already cited – ends her book with the claim that there is at least one fundamental right of animals: 'the right to be believed in' (Hearne 2007: 266). Perhaps she means this: when we recognize, as we must do when listening to an animal's being, that it has its own perspective – its own theatre of meaning, its own world – we should also recognize that this perspective is no less valid than ours. This is the third of the truths that is able to penetrate us through being with an animal. No one looking into a dog's eyes, or watching a cat hunt, or hearing a blackbird sing from a roof, can think that these creatures have somehow got the world wrong, that they – unlike us – fail to experience it as it really is. To 'believe in' the animal's perspective is not, of course, to privilege it above any other, but it is to acknowledge that the world becomes present to creatures in radically different ways, as so many different 'gifts' from the source of things. The *dao* – *the* way – 'gives' many ways of experience, none of them privileged.

To have a living sense of the existence of the many worlds of animals is at the same time to have a sense of the mystery of the world's being as it is – of its figuring for us as it does and not in any of the countless ways it figures for other beings. There can be no explanation of its presencing as it does for us since, to repeat, any attempted explanation would assume the exclusive truth of our perspective. And it is precisely the hubris of this assumption that being with animals dispels.

ANIMALS AND 'THE OPEN'

Throughout history, some animals have been credited with powers of insight, denied to ordinary human mortals, into the mysteries of being. In many traditional native religions, for example, the skills of the shaman include tapping into these animal powers so as to facilitate communication between the earthly and the divine. But the idea that animals may be equipped with a sense of mystery, in which we watchers of animals might then vicariously share, does not have to take any specifically religious form. If there is something to this idea, in whatever form, then there is a further way, additional to the one just discussed, in which engagement with animals may cultivate a sense of mystery.

The German poet Rainer Maria Rilke was fascinated by the eyes and gazes of animals; by the panther whose vision is 'exhausted' by looking through the bars of his cage, or by 'the golden amber of [the] eyeballs' of a black cat in which you see yourself, a tiny figure like 'a prehistoric fly'. In the eighth of his *Duino Elegies*, Rilke writes that 'animals look out into the Open', their faces 'tell[ing] us what exists', whereas our eyes are 'turned the other way' (Rilke 2004: 46ff). This is because, the poet explains in a letter, the animal, unlike us, does not 'place the world against itself'; it is thoroughly 'in' its world, not standing before or opposite it, as we do (in Heidegger 1971: 108).

Here, I think, is how we should understand Rilke's point. Human beings impose themselves on their world, not just through technological interventions, but through regimenting things under a scheme of concepts and through measuring and judging things according to their value and use for themselves. In the words of the Elegy, people 'overshadow' the world, and are always in the business of 'reconstructing' it according to their predilections. The animal's world, by contrast, is 'open', since it is 'unformulated' and 'unsupervised'. The animal, moreover, experiences the world 'without regard for who he is', so that, without an ego standing between it and the world, this experience is 'pure'. A cat or a crow, gazing out over the landscape in the late afternoon sun, is not constrained in advance to categorize and structure the scene in this or that way. Immersed in the immediate experience, the animal enjoys, Rilke's letter tells us, an 'indescribably open freedom'.

It is this freedom, this 'nearness to the Open', that for an admirer of Rilke, Martin Heidegger, is essential to inviting in 'the holy mystery' of things. We cannot, he explains, be open to a sense of mystery when we experience things only as 'subjected to the command of our self-assertive production', to the pragmatic imperatives that structure and condition the all-too-human world (Heidegger 1971: 111).

Do animals really look out into the Open and have a sense of the mystery of things? It's sometimes hard for me to dispel the feeling that they do when I look into the quiet, untroubled eyes of a cat or dog who looks past me into the distance, absorbed – so it seems – in something beyond my comprehension. But the lesson we might take from Rilke's poem does not depend on whether animals themselves really experience the sense of mystery that we hope to cultivate in ourselves. The real lesson is that we won't succeed in cultivating this unless we emulate the animals' 'open freedom' – their spontaneous receptivity to things, unconstrained by rigid conceptual schemes that limit how things may be experienced by us. The spontaneous, 'unsupervised' responses of animals testify to there being what one French observer of animals calls a 'reservoir' of possible experiences on which 'all creatures may draw'. It is, he adds, a reservoir from which human beings 'have learned to cut themselves off', through the artifices of culture, technology and science (Bailly 2011: 22). Another name for this reservoir might be the source – the ineffable source – of things.

Zhuangzi nostalgically recalls an age when 'people lived together with the birds and beasts'. There's been a loss and a decline, he makes clear, since we ceased, for the most part, to live in the company of animals (Zhuangzi 2009: Ch. 9). Zhuangzi's remarks on the spontaneity and naturalness of animals suggest that our separation from animals is complicit in the contrived, artificial lives most of us lead – lives that have all too little space in which to receive intimations of mystery, of the *dao*. The theme of spontaneity and receptivity to mystery is one that will recur in the pages ahead.

REFERENCES

Bailly, J.-C. 2011, *The Animal Side*, New York: Fordham University Press.

Derrida, J. 2008, *The Animal That Therefore I Am*, New York: Fordham University Press.

Hearne, V. 2007, *Adam's Task: Calling Animals by Name*, New York: Skyhorse.

Heidegger, M. 1971, What Are Poets For?, in *Poetry, Language, Thought*, New York: Harper & Row.

Ireland, J. (tr.) 1990, *The Udāna*, Kandy: Buddhist Publication Society.

James, S.P. 2009, *The Presence of Nature*, New York: Palgrave Macmillan.

Kundera, M. 1985, *The Unbearable Lightness of Being*, London: Faber & Faber.

Mann, T. 2003, *Bashan and I*, Pittsburgh, PA: University of Pennsylvania Press.

Merleau-Ponty, M. 2003, *Nature: Course Notes from the Collège de France*, Evanston, IL: Northwestern University Press.

Rilke, R.M. 2004, *Rilke's Late Poetry*, Vancouver: Ronsdale.

Uexküll, J. 2010, *A Foray into the World of Animals: with a Theory of Meaning*, Minneapolis, MN: University of Minnesota Press.

Zhuangzi. 2009, *Zhuangzi: The Essential Writings*, Indianapolis, IN: Hackett.

5

MUSIC

MUSIC AND EXPERIENCE

Going from the world of animals to the world of music looks like a large and sudden leap. But perhaps it isn't that huge. The twentieth-century French composer Olivier Messiaen remarked that, for him, 'the only real music' was 'in the sounds of nature', especially in the singing of birds (in Griffiths 2012: Ch. 10). That may be an eccentric view, but we could agree that 'the great animal orchestra of nature', as one musicologist calls it, is the origin of the music that human beings have come to create and enjoy (Krause 2012). Whether or not, at the end of the day, birdsong is labelled 'music' is less important than the fact that it is hard to hear it as being other than musical or music-like. What the blackbird on my roof emits has a rhythm, melody and tone that only someone deficient in musical sense could fail to hear.

People who deny that birds 'really' make music usually do so on the ground that they are producing sounds only for pragmatic purposes like attracting a mate, and not for purely aesthetic enjoyment. Even if this questionable claim about birds is true, the point registers a peculiarly modern and narrow conception of music. Music is being understood as one of 'the arts', the production of pieces of music to be experienced and enjoyed 'for their own sake', in concert halls, on iPods or whatever. But in nearly all societies over most of history, music has been integrated into larger practices – ritual, dance, warfare, work, magic, feasting and much else – and was not intended to be appreciated in isolation from its contribution to these practices. The art that we moderns now think of as music has derived from 'musicking', as one author dubbed the broad range of activities, including singing, dancing and playing instruments, that in all traditional societies have participated in the forms of social life (Small 1998).

So when I refer to musical experience, I am not thinking solely or mainly about aesthetic enjoyment of piano sonatas, jazz improvisations or pop songs. Musical experience is a larger engagement with, and participation in, musical environments, in contexts of many different kinds where music is performed, heard and used. Musical experience is as much *with* music as *of* it. Especially significant in traditional societies has been the interweaving of musical experience with engagement with the world of nature. And I'll soon be identifying some of the many ways in which the two forms of experience criss-cross and fuse.

The great Tang dynasty painter and poet, Wang Wei, describes how, when he returns to his 'old forest home' from the affairs of the city, he plays his zither in the moonlight. When he asks himself how the Way (*dao*) is to be achieved, he replies that it is by listening to a fisherman's song penetrating deep into a river bank (see Harris 2009: 224). His words nicely testify to an intersection between music and nature. But they do more than this, for they connect music and nature with attainment of the *dao*. Wang Wei's perception of a relation between song and river bank, he is suggesting, is an intimation of the way of things, of mystery. In what follows, I too will be proposing that experience of music in its intersection with nature may cultivate a sense of mystery. This is the sense, in particular, of what I earlier called the mystery of emergence. This was the mystery, not of the world's being just as it is, but of there being a world for us at all, the mystery of anything at all presencing for human experience.

This emphasis on music in relation to nature is faithful to my declared aim of trying to show how ways of engaging with nature cultivate a sense of mystery. But, apart from that, is there any good reason to restrict attention to this dimension of musical experience? After all, many claims have been made on behalf of music as such – of 'pure' musical sound, in isolation from the wider social world – to be a cipher of, or *entrée* to, realms of mystery. The music of Bach, Beethoven and others leads into 'the domain of the mystical'; brings us into 'the presence of the ineffable'; is heard as though it is 'breathed into the ear . . . from a higher sphere'. These are just a handful of the big claims made by composers, philosophers and musicologists about the spiritual power of music as such (see Cooper 2016a).

I don't want dogmatically to dismiss the possibility that dramatic experiences of great pieces of music might – like mystical 'visions' – provide some sort of acquaintance with the transcendent and ineffable. But I have the same reservations that I expressed about those visions. These dramatic musical experiences are too 'one-off', insufficiently integrated in the stream of a person's ordinary life, to provide an abiding sense of the mystery of things. Moreover, they are all too easy, after the event, to dismiss or pass off as illusory. It isn't uncommon even for resolute atheists to experience, in the presence of great religious music, feelings like those of the religiously devout. Later, however, over a drink in the pub, they shake these feelings off, and give no credence to what, in the cathedral or the concert hall, the sounds had seemed to convey.

Such dramatic musical experiences are, then, too staccato to inform, give an abiding tone to, and lend guidance to the ordinary conduct of life. The avant-garde composer and Zen Buddhist John Cage would agree. Music, he writes, should not be 'separate from the rest of life'; it should, in the familiar Zen idiom, be 'nothing special'. It is precisely because it is 'nothing special' that it may serve as a 'mise-en-scène for the emptiness of the Buddhist void', a 'skilful means' to 'arouse . . . wisdom [prajna]' as a quiet energy that courses through a person's everyday life (in Jaeger 2013: Chs 1–2). Cage sought in his music, writings and films to encourage an openness to our natural environment, including its ambient sounds. Like Wang Wei, he was aware of a deep affinity between musical experience and appreciation of nature. Let's follow the Chinese poet and the American composer here and articulate some of the important and intimate connections that exist between the two forms of experience.

MUSIC AND NATURE

Music may be dark, airy, heavy, sparkling, turbulent, sinuous, thundering. A piece of music may soar, peak, descend, drive forward or settle back. The natural world provides many metaphors for describing music, but the debt is repaid, for nature in turn is spoken of in musical terms. Elephants trumpet, whales sing, birds join in a dawn chorus, a jungle is a whole animal orchestra, a landscape is a great symphony, and nature has its own rhythms. This exchange of metaphors is some testimony to an affinity or convergence between musical experience and perceptions of nature – an affinity close enough for the two languages, of music and nature, to enrich one another.

The connections between music and nature are not, of course, confined to the realm of figurative descriptions. Indeed, what helps to make such descriptions possible are real-life experiences of convergence between musical practice and engagement with natural environments. Just handling or getting sounds out of a musical instrument can invite an appreciation of nature's contribution to music. Players of the Japanese shakuhachi flute record how the very feel of the knobbly bamboo root at the base of the instrument gives a sense of connection with the forest. One maker of Native American flutes describes how their 'wonderful music' makes him feel 'connected' with, and 'grateful' to, the trees from which they are made (Clifford 2012: Ch. 8). 'Connection' and 'gratitude' are terms that naturally occur in descriptions of the moods and feelings expressed in the musical rituals of traditional societies. The Native American rain-dancer dances with the elements whose cooperation he hopes to invite, and Black Elk recalls how, in the 'Elk Dance', he would change into an elk, thereby drawing on the powers represented by this animal (Neihardt 2014: 129).

Not all performances in which dancers or musicians cooperate with nature are undertaken with ritualistic or magical intentions. This isn't the intention when, for example, Wang Wei plays his zither in the moonlight by the river, or Henry David Thoreau plays his flute in the company of fish (Thoreau 1886: 173). Rather, the purpose – and the effect – is mutual enhancement of the experiences, respectively, of music-making and the natural environment in which the music sounds out. The legendary Yellow Emperor, Zhuangzi tells us, would adjust the music he played to the ambient sounds so as to enjoy a feeling of harmony with the landscape (Zhuangzi 2009: Ch. 14). In traditional societies, it is not only individual persons who 'jam' along with nature, but whole groups or tribes. The Kaluli people of Papua New Guinea, for example, gather together to make music that chimes with environmental sounds, such as the cries of animals.

There are other ways, besides jamming with nature, in which musicians cooperate with and employ natural sounds. Beethoven incorporates the sounds of the birds he heard on his walks in his 'Pastoral' Symphony, while in several works of Messiaen representation of birdsong is the central purpose. Many contemporary sound-artists do not represent the sounds of nature in their work, but record and incorporate them in their compositions. Other composers who aspire to bring music and appreciation of nature together have a different strategy. Claude Debussy dreamt of writing music specially for performance in the open air – music whose sounds would 'sport and skim among the tree tops' and thereby induce a sense of 'greater harmony with [the] natural scenery' (Debussy 1927: 32).

In these and many other ways, music and nature enter into communication, and musical practice and engagement with nature intersect. The examples I have given are enough to demonstrate kinds of convergence between music and nature that are especially relevant to our concern with the bearing of this relationship on a sense of mystery.

When Wang Wei listens to the fisherman's song at the same time as he watches the river bank and feels the evening breeze on his skin, his experience is a unitary one – not a set of separate perceptions that happen to be occurring at the same time. Asked to focus just on the song, and to ignore the breeze and the reeds on the bank, he would not be able to oblige. Or, at any rate, what he focuses on – the sounds – will have changed in character, and no longer be merged with, no longer inflected by, the other components in the total experience.

Most of us are familiar with experiences in which appreciation of the music is inseparable from that of a natural environment. Early one evening last summer, I sat on a shingle beach, with a salty breeze in my face, listening through earphones to Mendelssohn's Hebrides Overture and looking out towards a Hebridean island. A scientist may distinguish between the physical processes responsible for the auditory, olfactory, tactile and visual dimensions of the experience. But this doesn't mean that the experience of music-and-island-and-breeze-and-shingle is divisible into independent parts that then get stitched together.

Indeed, the moment I try to isolate an independent part – the sounds, say – it ceases to be the experience it was when merged with the rest. The components of the integrated experience belong to it not by being added together, but through mutual inflection. Had the sun come out, the music would have sounded different, just as, if I'd been listening to more gentle music, the island's mood would have changed. Indivisible into discrete parts, no explanation can be given in terms of such parts, or of anything else, of the emergence of the experience. My experience of music-and-island-and-breeze-and-shingle just came to be in spontaneous harmony.

To be sure, experiences like mine and Wang Wei's can only occur against a certain background. They are possible only for people who have grown up in a form of life where musical experience and engagement with nature have intersected and shaped one another. Theirs must be a form of life in which, palpably, culture and nature converge. The relationship between nature and culture is something I have already touched on and now want to revisit.

MUSIC, CULTURE, ENVIRONMENT

Musical and environmental experiences inflect one another not only on particular occasions in the lives of particular individuals but within the larger form of life – social, communal – in which these lives are embedded. The mutual inflection of music and environment is an example of the relationship between culture and nature. I've already proposed that this relationship is an intimate one, so much so that it is impossible to imagine cultural practices and perceptions of nature existing in isolation from one another. My argument, in Chapter 3, for this proposal was an abstract one: no descriptions and perceptions of the world are possible independently of human purposes, practices and perspectives, yet any particular practices in which we engage presuppose ways of experiencing nature, the world about us. The relationship between culture and nature is therefore a dynamic or dialectical one.

A main reason for considering how musical and environmental experiences inflect each other is to make this abstract conclusion come alive. We might tick as 'True' the statement that culture and nature are mutually dependent, but this is not to be in live confrontation with their interplay. And it is this that is needed if this interplay is to invite a sense of mystery. Engagement with musical practice and natural environments is one good way of promoting a feeling for what an ethnomusicologist has called 'the transformative play of nature and culture' (Feld 2009: 200).

That acquaintance with nature affects how music is heard may sound too obvious to remark upon. People won't hear a piece of music as depicting the rushing of waves or the power of a storm if they are without any experience of these natural phenomena. But there are more interesting, less apparent, ways in which music is shaped by environment. It's been said of Sibelius's music that it is 'the product of' and 'sprung fully grown from' the 'glacial boulders, lakes and forests' of Finland. Sea and forest are not so much represented in the Prelude to Debussy's *Pelléas et Mélisande*, it's been claimed, as 'present in [his] work': it is music 'penetrated by the mysterious power of nature'. Nature is not depicted but, according to the composer himself, 'finds a voice' in one of Mahler's symphonies. These are testimonies to how the composition of – and the hearing of – music may be a profound response to immersion in natural environments (see Cooper 2016b: 183ff).

Such responses, whether by the makers or the hearers of music, need not be at all 'highbrow'. The sea shanties, work songs, and religious chants of traditional communities can be properly heard and understood only by people who know the kinds of environment where the practices of fishing, farming and worship, to which the music gives voice, are located. It is, perhaps, in tribal societies, like that of the Kaluli, where music is made in unison or counterpoint with the ambient sounds of the landscape, that the inflection of music by nature is most pronounced.

But the inflection, here, is not just one-way, for tribal music often aims, as well, to encourage ways of perceiving the creatures and landscape that surround the village. A dance might, for example, portray an animal as brave or as demanding to be appeased. Sea shanties and work songs, too, do not just reflect, but influence, the experiences of place. The Mississippi or a Chinese paddy field doesn't look the same after hearing the songs of black slaves or rice pickers. Or, consider how film scores have helped to mould perceptions of and attitudes to animals and landscape. It's hard to travel through the American West without expectations and responses that have been prepared in advance by Westerns and documentaries whose scores evoke prairies, deserts and canyons. Musical accompaniment to films about animals has done much to shape our perception of some creatures as cute and cuddly, others as mean and crafty.

As these examples suggest, it is not the music alone that works to form or transform experience of nature, but music in combination with other cultural practices – film, literature, painting, ritual and so on. The same is true of the impact of 'serious' music on environmental perceptions. If Sibelius's symphonies and tone-poems were 'sprung' from the Finnish landscape, they have in turn helped to inflect the very way this landscape is envisaged – as dark, mysterious, brooding. But, of course, it is not the compositions alone that have done this: sagas, paintings, poems – these, too, have helped to 'construct' or render the Nordic landscape for us. Again, 'English Pastoral', to which a popular vision of the English countryside owes much, is not confined to the music of figures like Ralph Vaughan Williams, for it refers as well to traditions of poetry, the novel and landscape painting. Still, music plays its part – sometimes a major part – in the shaping of experiences of landscape and nature more generally.

Between a musical culture and people's engagement with nature, then, there is interdependence, mutual inflection. A person versed in a musical culture will find in it the traces of the environments in which the culture grew up. Just as people for whom aspects of their environment have special salience and significance will know that this owes, in part, to the way their culture has prepared them to experience the environment. Reflective experience of music in relation to nature is, in effect, to be directly acquainted with the dialectic between the two. It is a confrontation and confirmation through the senses of the truth of Maurice Merleau-Ponty's remark that 'it is impossible to say that nature ends here and that man or expression starts there' (Merleau-Ponty 2004: 319). It is impossible, for example, to say that the contribution to people's experience of Christmas of snowy landscapes and robins ends here and the contribution of carols, tinsel and roasting chestnuts starts here.

MUSIC AND THE MYSTERY OF EMERGENCE

If nature and 'man or expression' cannot be cordoned off from one another, then there is mystery in the emergence of a world – any world – that can be described and experienced. Since perceptions of culture and nature are mutually inflected, neither are autonomous. It is impossible, therefore, to explain the emergence of culture in terms of culture alone or to explain the emergence of nature in terms of nature alone. But nor is it possible to explain the emergence of one in terms of the other, for they are always already fused. There is no level of cultural description that does not already register perceptions of nature, and no level of nature description that does not already register human practice and perspective. So the emergence of a world – the presencing of anything for experience – cannot be explained or described. It is a mysterious upsurge, a coming to be, from a source that is itself mysterious.

Over the last few pages, I have been describing experiences of music/nature. The fusing of the words indicates the fusing of what they refer to. The point of the descriptions is to invoke experiences that give a sense of the mystery of emergence – that give life to the truth of the claim that there is indeed mystery here. Some of these experiences were 'occurent' ones – like Wang Wei's by the river bank, and mine on a shingle beach in Scotland – where it is impossible to separate out musical and environmental perceptions. Others are a more abiding recognition, in our encounters with music and nature, of a reciprocal shaping of perceptions, attitudes and responses. This is a recognition that is not confined to, but is especially sharp in, encounters with music performed in the very environments that are the cradles of the music – music that, in turn, has helped to transform how the places are understood and engaged with.

I want to say that experience or engagement with music/nature is a cipher of the emergence of world; it prompts awareness of an emergence that it exemplifies or epitomizes. Put differently, music/nature when authentically heard and engaged with is an epiphany of emergence. The experience or engagement with music/nature, it might be said, is 'semi-transparent' to the mystery of emergence (see Bennett-Hunter 2014: Ch. 6). For those who mindfully attend to the experience, it yields a faint and gentle intimation of the mysterious process whereby a world presences at all.

One good reason for thinking that experience of music/nature epitomizes and intimates the emergence of world is worth dwelling on. It is an experience that is constantly changing, developing, transforming. Not only do the themes of Mendelssohn's overture develop and change, so do the colours and tones of the island and the sea in front of me. Likewise, the mutual inflections of musical practice and environmental perception are constantly altering and modifying. An experience of music/nature, then, is not something that suddenly pops up and freezes; it is in process and movement all the time it endures. And this is what should be said, too, of a world that emerges; as a totality that becomes present for experience, it perpetually changes and transforms. A world is not a 'creation' – something set up and left to look after itself – by some creator. It is all the time coming to be, a seamless thematic development like that of a melody or whole symphony.

Experience of music/nature is an epiphany of the emergence of worlds as this is conceived in various Asian traditions. The term *dao*, it's helpful to remember, has a verbal, 'active' sense; it can mean 'to lead' or 'to cut a path' or 'to make a way'. If, as for Daoists, the *dao* is the source from which worlds emerge, these worlds are themselves 'ways', courses of flux and movement, like waterways. If the *dao* 'gives' worlds, then the gifts are not ready-made, complete objects, like children's toys, but more like the gift of children themselves – the gift of what is ever growing, forming and re-forming.

Engagement with music/nature is an epitome, too, of how the emergence of world is thought of in some Buddhist traditions. A world is 'empty'; it is not one big 'object' and it is devoid of 'substances' or things with 'own-being' and 'permanence'. Instead, it is a constant process of 'dependent origination', a continual flux or 'conflagration' in which everything is caught up. The emergence of a world at all is a mystery, for there is nothing – that is, no thing, no entity – that could account for its coming into being. Perhaps this is what John Cage had in mind when thinking of music as 'a *mise-en-scène* for the emptiness of the Buddhist void'. Music is, as it were, an environment or space we can occupy, one in which we may receive intimations of the arising of a world from emptiness, the condition for anything to emerge at all. This is why Cage could entertain the hope that engagement with music and nature might 'arouse [the] *prajna* – intuitive wisdom/energy' that Buddhism seeks to nurture.

Cage, we noted, emphasized that music should be 'nothing special' and integrated with ordinary life. So if music is to 'arouse' wisdom, this is not through conjuring up awesome visions or inducing paranormal states of consciousness. In 1948, Cage wrote a piece for a prepared piano, 'In a Landscape'. This is a gentle piece that, although it is composed in a modernist idiom, is lyrical, even pastoral. It is best listened to in the kind of tranquil natural environment that it evokes, a kind Cage would often invite us to spend time in. When it is heard in this context, the piece is an epitome of the confluence of human invention and receptivity to nature that has been the subject of this chapter. We should accept Cage's invitation to listen to music alongside the ambient sounds of nature. Doing so is a way of coming to sense the mystery of emergence.

REFERENCES

Bennett-Hunter, G. 2014, *Ineffability and Religious Experience*, London: Pickering & Chatto.

Clifford, C.H. 2012, *Wilderness Rhythms*, Kindle ed.

Cooper, D.E. 2016a, Music, Nature and Ineffability, *Philosophia*, Jan 2016, doi:10.1007/s1146-015-9656-9.

Cooper, D. E. 2016b, Music and the Presence of Nature, in B. Bannon (ed.), *Nature and Experience: Phenomenology and the Environment*, New York: Rowman & Littlefield, pp. 175–86.

Debussy, C. 1927, *M. Croche: The Dilettante Hater*, London: Viking.

Feld, S. 2009, Lift-Up-Over Sounding, in D. Rothenberg and M. Ulvaeus (eds), *The Book of Music and Nature*, Middleton, CT: Wesleyan University Press, pp. 193–206.

Griffiths, P. 2012, *Olivier Messiaen and the Music of Time*, London: Faber, Kindle ed.

Harris, P. (ed.) 2009, *300 Tang Poems*, New York: Knopf.

Jaeger, P. 2013, *John Cage and Buddhist Ecopoetics*, London: Bloomsbury, Kindle ed.

Krause, B. 2012, *The Great Animal Orchestra: Finding the Origins of Music in the World's Wild Places*, London: Profile.

Merleau-Ponty, M. 2004, Eye and Mind, in T. Baldwin (ed.), *Maurice Merleau-Ponty: Basic Writings*, London: Routledge.

Neihardt, J.G. 2014, *Black Elk Speaks: The Complete Edition*, Lincoln, NB: University of Nebraska Press.

Small, C. 1998, *Musicking: The Meanings of Performing and Listening*, Middletown, CT: Wesleyan University Press.

Thoreau, H.D. 1886, *Walden*, London: Scott.

Zhuangzi. 2009, *Zhuangzi: The Essential Writings*, Indianapolis, IN: Hackett.

6

WALKING

MEDITATION ON THE MOVE

Henry David Thoreau, I mentioned, enjoyed playing his flute outdoors in the company of fish. He also enjoyed walking, lamenting the fact that he knew only two or three people who really 'understood the art . . . of taking walks', or 'sauntering' as he called it. Walking, for Thoreau, wasn't, however, simply a form of enjoyment and exercise. Through sauntering he hoped to experience 'a great awakening light', and the paths he walked were 'symbolical' of the one that leads to an 'ideal world' (Thoreau 2012: 3, 7, 27, 52).

Thoreau is not alone in his confidence that walking is a means to spiritual understanding. In the autumn of 2014, an exhibition titled *Walking Poets* was mounted in the Wordsworth museum, located next to the poet's home in the English Lake District. For Wordsworth himself, he explains in *The Prelude*, 'wandering' enabled him to 'meditate in peace' in search of knowledge (Wordsworth 1984: 572), as it did for the other poet paired with Wordsworth in the exhibition – the seventeenth-century Japanese writer and traveller, Matsuo Bashō. 'Walking poet', or 'meditator on the move', is an apt term, as well, for other writers and prodigious walkers associated with these two poets – for Wordsworth's collaborator, Samuel Taylor Coleridge, for example, and the twelfth-century poet and fellow-Buddhist whom Bashō greatly admired, Saigyō (see Cooper 2017).

What I have in mind by meditation on the move is not any of the disciplined, demanding, purposeful and sharply focused practices of walking familiar in various religions. It's not, for example, the 'walking Zen' that punctuates periods of seated meditation with slow, concentrated walking around a garden or a hall. Bashō tells us that his walks had 'no rules', and he went where he pleased, without any fixed itinerary (Bashō 1966: 85). These are the kind of walks that Thoreau described as 'sauntering'. They are not walks undertaken for solely practical reasons – to get to the post office or the local pub, say. Nor, at the other extreme, is meditative walking a mobile form of intense inner scrutiny. Thoreau expresses impatience with self-absorbed people who pay no attention to the wood through which they are walking. They are, he writes, 'out of [their] senses', unconnected with their environment (Thoreau 2012: 10).

The title of Jean-Jacques Rousseau's final, and posthumously published, work is *Reveries of a Solitary Walker*. Revery, for Rousseau, is not idle day-dreaming, but nor is it rational deliberation or introspective gazing into the recesses of the soul. In revery, rather, the walker's ideas 'follow their own bent without constraint', and 'the soul rambles and glides through the universe'. With 'passions and practical concerns suspended', the walker 'forgets himself' (Rousseau 1992: 91ff).

The terminology and the thought here are strikingly like those of Zhuangzi, two thousand years earlier, when describing and praising what his translators have variously called 'rambling', 'roaming' and 'wandering'. The rambler is 'unfettered', liberated from the opposition of 'self and other', and hence is 'carried along by things so that the heart-mind wanders freely' (Zhuangzi 2009: Ch. 4). Rambling, for Zhuangzi and Rousseau alike, is a relaxed yet mindful style of walking. It is also a metaphor for a spontaneity of the spirit and a responsiveness to the world that this style of walking enables. Meditation on the move is an exercise, in effect, of the paramount Daoist virtue of *ziran* – 'self-so-ness', spontaneity, naturalness – that is held to mimic the *dao* itself.

The Sri Lankan garden I described at the beginning of this book was one that I was not only located in, but walking in. This was as important to the sense of mystery afforded by the evening as the sounds, smells, textures and sights that surrounded me. We may not ordinarily think of awareness of the movement of one's own body through space and along the ground as a form of sensory perception. But it belongs alongside vision, hearing and the rest as a mode in which our environment becomes present for us.

It's been said that the environment – indeed, nature at large – was Wordsworth's office. Certainly it was when striding up hills, following the course of a river, walking on rural paths, or simply pacing back and forth in his own garden that he was especially susceptible to feeling an 'undetermined sense of unknown modes of being' or a 'sentiment of Being spread o'er all that moves' (Wordsworth 1984: 385, 402). Wordsworth, of course, is not alone in finding that walking – meditation on the move – provides intimations of mystery. Those who share his view are right, I'll argue, to find that walking has this power. But before directly addressing the relationship between walking and senses of mystery, let's ask how it is that walking is conducive to revery, spontaneity and flexibility of the spirit.

BODY, MIND AND INVOLVEMENT

Why should walking and wandering through landscapes be so hospitable to revery, to meditation of the sort I described? Part of the answer must be that the supple, relaxed motion of the body of the good walker induces analogous mental qualities. 'My wit does not budge', remarked Michel de Montaigne, 'if my legs are not moving' (Montaigne 1991: 933). Nietzsche concurs: 'do not give credence to any thought that was not born outdoors while one moved about freely – in which the muscles are not celebrating a feast, too' (Nietzsche 1968: 696). It is as if springiness of step is inherited by the walker's thoughts and imagination. The mind, it seems, is carried along by the same flow of energy that courses through the walker's body. Part of the answer, too, must be that walking constantly supplies the walker with changing vistas, novel scenes, new sounds and smells. For the walking poet, like Wordsworth or Bashō, these serve as symbols, fresh materials for revery, food for the imagination. In my study at home, nothing happens; there are no processes of change to carry my thought along with them. The study is a place for dogged deliberation or for lazy day-dreams, not for the spontaneity of revery.

But there's a more interesting explanation of why walking is conducive to meditation. There are many degrees, both bodily and cognitive, of involvement with natural environments. Walking has just the right degrees of involvement to inspire revery. Consider, first, the many grades of people's bodily involvement with environment. These range from climbing a vertical rock face to lying on one's back in a meadow below the rock. The former demands total bodily control and focus, allowing no room for meditative revery. The climber who does indulge in this is likely to fall off the rock face. Lying in the meadow, by contrast, requires no bodily prowess and concentration, and hence makes space for revery. But it makes space for a lot more as well – anxieties, fantasies and obsessive self-analysis, for example. Lying there, I want my thoughts to float free like the clouds drifting above, but instead, I worry about losing my job or my girlfriend, or about a proneness to lose my temper too easily.

Walking is nicely situated between these extremes of bodily involvement. Rambling does not demand the concentration and physical prowess of the rock climber, but it does – unlike lying in the meadow – require attention to the body and its environment, to gradients, potholes, stones, hornet nests or whatever. The walker who ignores these is liable to trip, stagger, get puffed out or stung. As a historian of walking elegantly expresses it, walking requires us to 'be in our bodies and in the world without being made busy by them' – not so busy, at any rate, as to exclude the possibility of revery (Solnit 2014: Ch. 1).

Consider, next, the many degrees of people's intellectual or cognitive involvement with environments. At one end of the scale there is the focused, detailed examination of an environment by a landscape archaeologist or botanist. At the other end of the scale, someone in training for a marathon may run along the road that bisects this environment without taking any notice at all of the trees, fields and hills that lie on either side. Walking or rambling, once again, is in the mean between these extremes. For the walker, unlike the marathon runner, the environment is present, something to be alert to and mindful of. Unlike the archaeologist or botanist, however, the walker's perceptions of the environment are not dictated by specific professional objectives – to discover some buried pottery, say, or find a rare species of fern among the rocks. The walker has no programme. No rules, Bashō told us, compelled or constrained what he would notice and appreciate as he walked the old roads of Japan.

This does not mean that nothing is yielded to the walker, that no understanding of natural environments is gained through meditative revery. But what is yielded is liable to be very different from what the professional seeker of knowledge – the scientist – is after. When Bashō stops to look at an old cherry tree, 'many things of the past . . . are brought to [his] mind' (Bashō 1966: 79). But these are almost certainly not the same things that come to the attention of the landscape archaeologist or botanist in the course of their research.

This raises the question of what modes of understanding of the world, what ways of experiencing it, are encouraged, invited in or given vitality by meditation on the move.

COMMUNION AND HOLISM

A leisurely trawl through the writings of the walking poets – Wordsworth, Coleridge, Thoreau, Bashō and many others – shows that it is three experiences that, above all, are inspired by meditative walking. These are the senses of communion with the natural world, of the unity of nature, and of the mystery of things. I want to begin by looking at the first two since it is through them that a sense of mystery is nurtured.

Thoreau speaks for his fellow walking poets when declaring that sauntering induces a feeling of being 'part and parcel of nature'. So does Wordsworth's sister Dorothy when she cele-brates, one sunny day, how the landscape is 'allied to human life' (Wordsworth 2012: 20). An experience of convergence between human practice and the natural world was also a main theme in the earlier chapter on music. The experiences with which we're now concerned are, however, prompted in a different way.

The walker, unlike the rock climber, is not preoccupied with his or her body – with the placing of the feet, say, or a dis-tribution of its weight. Yet the walker certainly has a sense of body, especially – though not only – when it tires or is afflicted by rain or a burning sun. The walker can't forget the body in the way that I usually can when sitting quietly and immobile in my study. There is a constant, though usually muted, sense of the body's relationship to the ground that is walked and to the landscape through which it moves. The environment is not gazed out at from the two eye sockets of a head; rather, it is constantly engaged with by a moving body. This environment is not, like a big cinema screen, observed as an object set before, or over against, the person who engages with it. And when the walker enjoys a landscape, it is not, typically, as a being detached from some object that it contemplates across a divide. The enjoyment is that of someone who participates in, belongs to, what is appreciated. Or better, this participation – this belonging – is an aspect of what is appreciated. The body and its movement in the landscape – its being 'part and parcel' of it – is a source of the walker's satisfaction and delight.

Between the meditative walker and the landscape there is no confrontation. On the contrary, it was essential to the meditation on the move described by Rousseau and Zhuangzi that the walker is 'carried along', effortlessly, by the surrounding things and places, freely 'roaming' from one spot to another. The walker imposes no fixed route on the landscape, as if it were an obstacle course to battle through. Meditative walking is marked by spontaneity and supple responsiveness to the surroundings – the very opposite to a stand-off between perceiving subjects and a world that confronts them. (The communion that we speak of as existing between two lovers is likewise marked by the spontaneity of their responses to one another.)

It's because of this close communion between walker and environment that walking poets, such as Coleridge, speak of a loss of self or individuality when they wander through landscapes. This is not perhaps a happy way of speaking, suggestive as it is of some big metaphysical event, the dissolution of an entity – the self – into an ocean of anonymity. One reason this is not a happy way of putting things is that it overlooks the role that the individual walker plays in shaping how the surrounding world becomes present to experience. The route I choose, the vantage-points at which I pause, the knowledge, interests and moods I bring along with me – these and much else about me will contribute to how the landscape figures for me. Just as it was impossible to separate out the responsibilities of music and nature for how places are experienced, so it is impossible to separate out those of walker and environment. This dialectic between walker and landscape is real and important, but it is overwrought and misleading to express it in terms of loss of selfhood.

A feeling of communion between walkers and environments is an ingredient in the larger sense of the unity of the natural world to which our walking poets also testify. This holistic sense is expressed by Wordsworth and Coleridge in their several references to 'the one life' that courses through things, and by Saigyō in verses that record the poet's perception of the deep relatedness and 'higher order unity of things'.

But how does meditation on the move encourage an experience of unity? A clue to the answer is the point already made about the walker's contribution to shaping and structuring the experience of a landscape. It is a point for which one author provides an apt image when she describes walking as 'mov[ing] through space like a thread in a fabric, sewing it together into a continuous experience' (Solnit 2014: Ch. 1). The walker, in effect, is making a motley of experiences of an environment into a coherent whole, within which items are understood in relation to one another. Seemingly unconnected things – trees, hills, ponds, streams, deer – become a landscape, an integrated whole where they are brought or 'sewn' together. The walker takes a path alongside a wood that leads up towards the top of a hill; having climbed the hill, the walker listens to a stream that descends to a pond below; descending the hill, the walker watches deer drinking from the pond, and observes the tracks made by their feet that lead to the wood where the walk began. The walker has gathered all of this into a coherent experiential whole.

And there's another aspect to gathering. For the mindful walker, the very items encountered – trees, deer and so on – are experienced as gathering around them the world in which they have their place and identity (see Heidegger 1971). The meditative walker sees the trees as gathering the soil in which they have their roots, the sun and rain that make them grow, the deer that eat their fruit, and the walkers who rest in the shade of their branches. For anything to be – to stand out as – a tree, a pond, a deer, it must gather about it the wholes within which it can be identified and appreciated as what it is: a node or 'knot' within a relational web. A tiny island in a lake is seen by Dorothy Wordsworth, in her poem 'Floating Island at Hawkshead', as a whole little 'world', a place where birds, plants, 'sky, lake . . . sunshine and storm, whirlwind and breeze' all gather and 'agree' with one another in a harmonious whole (in Wu 1994: 501).

To experience a landscape as an integrated whole might not be anything as grand or dramatic as a vision of the whole of reality being the 'manifold One', as the Romantics envisaged it. There is, after all, 'nothing special' in the experience. But a landscape experienced in this way is a cipher, a symbol, of how the world as a whole comes to presence. It is an invitation to acquire a holistic sense of this world.

WALKING AND SENSES OF MYSTERY

The meditative walker experiences communion with natural environments, ones that are perceived, moreover, as structured, relational wholes. How does this experience and perception modulate into senses of mystery?

The appreciation of environments by meditators on the move involves, we saw, awareness of their own relationship to the environments. The landscape is not enjoyed as some big spectacle separate from the walkers, but as a context in which their bodies and movements participate, one they are 'part and parcel' of. It is enjoyed as well as a context that is partly of the walkers' own making, as they 'sew' the various parts of the environment together. Their walking gathers trees, ponds, paths and animals into patterns and structures of meaning that have no existence independently of the walkers. Who knows how the landscape might figure for, and be organised by, creatures with very different sensibilities, enthusiasms and assumptions from those of walkers like ourselves?

What this indicates is that the meditative walker is confronted by the mystery of emergence. Just as it was impossible to separate out the contributions of cultural practice and environmental perception to the experience either of music or of nature, so it is in the case of meditative walking and the impingement of the environment. Perhaps this is not surprising, for the kind of walking that has concerned us in this chapter is itself a cultural practice. It is not simply a matter of placing one foot before another; rather, it is a practice replete with hopes, presuppositions and tastes that have been shaped by the traditions with which a person has grown up. How the landscape figures for the walker, how it becomes present, can't be due just to the landscape, as if it were already laid out in a determinate fashion. Nor, of course, can it be due simply to the imagination and initiative of the walker. The gathering together of things into a coherent, integrated environment through which the walker moves is a coming to presence that cannot be dissected and explained. To experience this gathering is to experience a mystery of emergence, an epitome of that larger coming to presence that is the human world as a whole.

The gathering together of things, we saw, was more than something achieved by the walker. Things as they are experienced themselves gather around them the environments in which they have their place and identity. The entire world, wrote the Zen master Dōgen, 'manifests itself in a tall bamboo' (Dōgen 1996: 89). Here he gives voice to the Buddhist doctrine of 'emptiness', at least as it is construed by several Chinese and Japanese schools. No thing, no object, has 'own-being', since it is what it is only in relation to everything else in the world – rather as a word has the meaning it does only through belonging to a complete language. The point is often illustrated by images of things such as bubbles and droplets that are not only fragile and ephemeral, but also reflect and are transparent to whatever is around them. To the enlightened understanding, everything is like a bubble in this respect.

But we don't just look through things to other things that gather about them. As one Buddhist text puts it, we 'look through each being' to 'suchness' – to the source, the ground, of all beings (Conze 1990: 217). Where there is 'true emptiness', maintained the Buddhist thinker, Nāgārjuna, there is 'wondrous being' (in Mitchell 1998: 289). The enlightened person performs, as it were, a feat of 'double exposure', 'tak[ing] in at a glance [and] as one Reality' both the realm of 'suchness' and 'the world of particular' objects (Suzuki 1934: 256). You see the tree or deer for what it is – a node in an experiential network of relations – but at the same time see this network, this world, as the gift of the ineffable source of things. The sense of the mystery of emergence that the gathering of trees, deer and ponds into an environmental whole conveys has become a sense, as well, of the mystery of the source. Once the world as a whole is experienced as mysteriously emerging, it is impossible to resist an intimation of a mysterious well-spring from which it emerges. We can't imagine it emerged, 'just like that', from nothing at all.

But can we, a sceptic will complain, really credit meditation on the move with the power to teach and instil truths of such profundity? It helps to weaken the force of this complaint to introduce a point made by several walking poets and by others who write in praise of walking. It's not, they want to say, that walking somehow communicates to people truths of which they were previously ignorant, that it teaches a lesson in metaphysics to the philosophically naive. When Zhuangzi recommends that we walk in 'a vast mountain forest', this is because it can 'reopen' the mind. It 'unblocks' the 'apertures' through which human beings were once receptive to the way of things – so that we may again 'wander in the Heavenly' (Zhuangzi 2009: Ch. 26). His point is that openness to the mysteries of emergence and source is, as it were, the default, original condition of human beings. It is a condition from which they have fallen. As men and women have become ever more subject to the constraints of complex economies, sophisticated technologies, systems of scientific knowledge, cultural and intellectual fashions, and the frenetic business of city life, their sense of mystery has atrophied. Meditation on the move is a journey of recollection, freeing men and women up for the vision of things that their more innocent, but wiser, ancestors once enjoyed.

Zhuangzi's point is echoed by our walking poets. It is in order to 'pursue the Way' that Buddhist poets like Saigyō and Bashō speak of a need to 'throw away' and 'abandon the secular world'. Only then can there be a retrieval of a sense of the Buddha-nature, the 'original' ground of everything that has become occluded for most of us by our grasping desires and the frenetic business of the world. Wordsworth, too, takes up this theme of recollection and retrieval; it is because, as the first line of his sonnet puts it, 'the world is too much with us' that, 'getting and spending' and 'lay[ing] waste our powers', we are no longer receptive to the sacred (Wordsworth 1984: 270). His own prodigious walks were ways to renew this receptivity.

The walking poets are not trying to teach us new philosophical lessons. The aim of the meditative walking that the poets recommend to us is to help us gain, or rather regain, a vital feeling for the truths that their poems evoke. Similarly, my purpose in this chapter has not been to convince you of the mysteries of world, emergence and source. My case for the existence of these mysteries was stated much earlier. The purpose, instead, has been to recommend a way – the way of meditative walking – through which ciphers and epitomes of these mysteries may be experienced. The walker alert to the body's relationship to an environment, to having a role in the formation of landscapes where things gather into coherent wholes, is thereby at least open to, and poised to recall and receive, intimations of mystery.

REFERENCES

Bashō. 1966, *The Narrow Road to the Deep North and Other Travel Sketches*, London: Penguin.

Conze, E. (ed.) 1990, *Buddhist Texts Through the Ages*, Boston: Shambhala.

Cooper, D.E. 2017, Meditation on the Move: Walking, Nature, Mystery, in P. Cheyne (ed.), *Coleridge and Contemplation*, Oxford: Oxford University Press.

Dōgen. 1996, *Shobogenzo*, Vol ii, London: Windbell.

Heidegger, M. 1971, The Thing, in *Poetry, Language, Thought*, New York: Harper & Row.

Mitchell, D. (ed.) 1998, *Masao Abe: A Zen Life of Dialogue*, Boston: Tuttle.

Montaigne, M. de 1991, *The Complete Essays*, London: Penguin.

Nietzsche, F. 1968, Ecce Homo, in *Basic Writings of Nietzsche*, New York: Modern Library.

Rousseau, J.-J. 1992, *Reveries of a Solitary Walker*, Indianapolis, IN: Hackett.

Solnit, R. 2014, *Wanderlust: A History of Walking*, London: Granta.

Suzuki, D.T. 1934, *Essays on Zen Buddhism*, III, London: Luzac.

Thoreau, H.D. 2012, *Walking*, Public Domain Book, Kindle ed.

Wordsworth, D. 2012, *The Grasmere and Alfoxden Journals*, Oxford: Oxford University Press.

Wordsworth, W. 1984, *William Wordsworth: A Critical Edition of the Major Works*, Oxford: Oxford University Press.

Wu, D. (ed.) 1994, *Romanticism: An Anthology*, Oxford: Blackwell.

Zhuangzi. 2009, *Zhuangzi: The Essential Writings*, Indianapolis, IN: Hackett.

7

GARDENING

THE WAY OF THE GARDEN

This book began in a garden. That garden was, like many others, a site hospitable to experiences of the kinds I have been discussing over the last three chapters. It was a garden where animals were seen, music was heard, and paths were walked. But over the pages that follow, my concern is not primarily with gardens as places to stroll through or sit in, or as creations to be admired or criticized. It is, rather, with the practice of gardening – of making, modifying, stocking and tending gardens. It is a practice, I'll be proposing, that may and should inspire a sense of mystery.

In Western countries, gardening is often regarded as a hobby, a recreation, albeit a practical one that yields useful products – vegetables to eat, flowers to enjoy. Most garden writing tends to consist either in practical advice to gardeners or in aesthetic appreciation of gardens. In East Asian countries, by contrast, gardening has been considered as a 'Way' (Chinese *dao*, Japanese *dō*, as in judō). A Way is certainly not a hobby, nor is it simply a skill or art. It is a practice of self-cultivation, and in some traditions a means of enlightenment. Gardening is a Way of 'bio-spiritual' cultivation − a practice, or group of practices, whereby the virtues of body and spirit are acquired and exercised. The good gardener is adept, supple, dextrous and graceful; but he or she is also clean, humble, considerate and self-disciplined. Bio-spiritual cultivation embraces what we modern Westerners rather artificially segregate into the bodily, moral and spiritual virtues (see Kirkland 2004: Ch. 2).

Ways whose practitioners manifest such virtues are routes to the achievement of harmony, the paramount aim of many East Asian spiritual traditions. Respectful care for shrine gardens, for example, brings people into 'fellowship with the kami', the divine forces that, for followers of Shinto, hold sway over the world (Kasulis 2004: 32, 36). More generally, Ways serve to integrate people into some larger whole, and eventually to what Daoists call 'the ultimate way of things'. One reason that Daoists, Zen Buddhists and others accord such importance to practising Ways is that the 'ultimate way', the ground of things, is ineffable. Since there can be no conceptual articulation of what is necessarily mysterious, great value attaches to practices that manifest an implicit understanding of, a feel for, the mysterious.

It shouldn't be a surprise that in these traditions gardening is among the most honoured of the various Ways. In China and Japan, analogies were perceived between human development and that of plants, so that there are instructive parallels between self-cultivation and the growing of flowers and vegetables. Several authors, moreover, employed the garden as a metaphor for the cosmos, comparing the Way of the gardener to the proper conduct of our lives in the wider world. People were encouraged to regard the garden as the world in miniature. What better education can there be for becoming 'gardeners of the cosmos', who take responsibility for shaping their lives and environments, than nourishing and tending living beings in their gardens? Humility, respect, patience, hope, attentiveness, self-discipline, sensitivity to beauty – these are among the virtues that the Way of the garden is especially apt to foster, and ones that are readily exported to the world beyond the garden wall (see Cooper 2015).

In Daoist, Buddhist and Shintoist sacred places, monks and priests take seriously their responsibilities for the gardens in which temples or shrines are set. Indeed, in China and Japan, many of the most celebrated garden makers were monks or priests. This is an indication of the connection made in these traditions between the Way of the garden and spiritual truth, between the practice of gardening and a sense of the mystery of things. A remarkable German woman who lived in Japan and mastered kadō (the Way of flowers, ikebana) wrote that in and through her art there was 'waiting to be experienced the mystery and deep ground of existence' (Herrigel 1999: 119). It is a remark echoed not only by fellow practitioners of kadō, including her teachers, but by many people whose horticultural world is more expansive than a vase of flowers – by gardeners, that is, who work with whole beds of flowers and much else.

That the garden may be a cipher of spiritual reality is not a thought confined to China and Japan. In Renaissance Italy, for example, theologians and garden designers alike spoke of the garden as a miniature 'book of God' – a place which, if 'read' properly, gave clues to the nature and purpose of the divine creator. With its symmetrical forms, for instance, a well-designed garden achieves 'congruence' or harmony with the divine mind. More generally, a large body of poetry attests to a perception that God is at work in the garden. But it is, perhaps, distinctive of East Asian traditions that it is the practice of gardening rather than the finished product – the activity rather than what is acted upon – that intimates or 'bodies forth' the ground of things. Be that as it may, let's ask how gardening is a Way with the capacity to cultivate a sense of mystery. Why is it

a Way especially suited to promoting a feeling for the presence
and workings of the way, the *dao*?

GARDENS AND MEANING

In fact, I'll pause a bit before considering how gardening is distinctive in its power to promote a sense of mystery. I want first
briefly to compare experience of gardens with the kinds of experience discussed in the chapters on music in relation to nature
and meditative walking. Gardens, I suggest over the next couple
of pages, have the same general significance for the truth of mystery as do music and walking.

When it is asked what meaning a garden has, there can be
several types of answer. A hotel garden will have an emotional
significance for the couple who spent many hours of their hon-
eymoon seated there. Japanese gardens are often deliberate rep-
resentations of famously beautiful natural environments. Or,
like Thomas Jefferson's Monticello, a garden may have historical
significance, as an expression of a moral creed – of republican
virtues of self-reliance and liberty, in his case. Or the purpose of
a garden may be to commemorate the dead. One and the same
garden can have meanings of many different sorts – personal,
representational, historical, emotional and so on. So, at one level,
there is no such thing as the meaning of gardens, of the garden
as such. Still, it is worth exploring whether gardens in general
share a certain significance for human beings, whether there is
something that they exemplify or epitomize.

A familiar feature of Chinese and Japanese gardens is the
moon-bridge that arches over a stream. Above the stream is the
man-made creation, in stone or wood; below the bridge is its
reflection in the flowing water. Looked at from an appropriate
angle, the bridge and its reflection form a perfect circle. It's hard
to think of a more apt symbol of union between human artifice
and nature. But, then, the garden as a whole itself exemplifies

this unity, this 'dialectic' between culture and nature. Gardens point to, signify, this unity, and they do so more saliently, and more obviously, than music and walking did.

Certainly, mindful experience of the garden is marked by the mutual inflections between culture and nature that we encountered when reflecting on music and walking. We discovered, for example, that it was impossible in the case of some musical experiences to separate out the contributions of the music heard and the natural environment in which it is heard. Similarly, appreciation of a garden does not, typically, split apart into admiration for the contributions of the gardener and of nature respectively. My appreciation doesn't switch backwards and forwards between, say, the flowers themselves and the taste or expertise with which they have been planted. My enjoyment is not the result of welding together two distinct experiences, any more than my enjoyment of *Swan Lake* is the product of separate pleasures taken in the music and in the dancing.

Between the gardener and nature there are countless physical, causal interactions. The disappearance of the patch of nettles is due to the gardener's scythe; the disappearance of a greenhouse to a great storm. More interesting, however, are the ways in which the gardener's actions shape perceptions of natural environments, and vice versa. A famous Japanese treatise on gardening instructs gardeners to heed 'the request of the stone' – in other words, to reflect on and respond to the character of the materials they work with before they make or modify their gardens (Takei and Keane 2001: 4). In turn, however, the placing of the stone will influence the look of the surrounding landscape – drawing attention, say, to shapes in the hills that resemble the stone's. Or, in a manner analogous to the 'gathering' of things into experiential wholes for the walker, the placing of the stone may draw plants or other stones towards it so as to provide form and coherence to an area of the garden. Or think of the way in which eighteenth-century English gardeners, inspired by Chinese gardens, would 'borrow scenery' from the environment, so as to enhance the look of a garden or affect its mood.

Mutual inflection doesn't occur only at the level of the individual garden, for whole styles of garden making and shared conceptions of the natural world may inform one another. The highly formal gardens of Renaissance Italy and Louis XIV's France were intended to contrast favourably with the rude wildness of natural landscapes that had not been commandeered for human use. They served, thereby, to reinforce the idea of wildness as alien to the divinely ordered rational structure of the universe that the gardener sought to represent. By contrast, today's opposed perception of nature – as a fragile system threatened by hubristic technologies – is reflected in, and heightened by, gardens that eschew formalism and other assertions of human domination of nature.

I could, as I have done elsewhere (Cooper 2006), elaborate on this, but enough has been said to show that gardens testify no less – and indeed more emphatically – than music and walking do to the inseparability of culture and nature. If the garden, as the Chinese poets urged, should be regarded as the cosmos in miniature, then the lesson it teaches is that the world is a human world. The world as it can be experienced is not just 'there', already set out and waiting for us to encounter it. But nor is it simply our invention, a fiction. What the metaphor of the world as a garden conveys is Zhuangzi's insight that, despite our urge to do so, there is no sense finally to separating out what is 'done by the human' and what is done by heaven and earth (Zhuangzi 2009: Ch. 6). But to recognize this is already close to acknowledging that the world – culture-and-nature together – inexplicably emerge. It should not cause any surprise, therefore, to read that the Daoist garden, in its own quiet way, helps to make possible 'the inexpressible experience of the *dao*' (Keswick 1980: 82).

But we have yet to identify how the Way of the garden does involve this experience.

'IN THE HEAD' AND 'IN THE HANDS'

It is easy to misunderstand the way in which a sense of mystery is related to music, walking, gardening and other practices. It's tempting to think of this sense as an 'inner' psychological state – a belief, perhaps, or a vision – that is the effect of a day spent singing, walking, or working in the garden. This misunderstanding is of a piece with the exaggeration of the place of belief – of doctrines and 'cognitive' states – in religious understanding that I criticized in Chapter 3. Like the religious sense, a sense of mystery is located in people's practices and engagements with the world, not something that pops into their heads or souls as a result of these. To recall Wittgenstein's remark, religion is a way of living and 'assessing life'. Something similar should be said about a sense of mystery. Rather as a pianist's understanding of a piece of music is shown by how he or she plays it, so an appreciation of mystery is shown in and through ways of engaging with the world. This was one reason why it was important to emphasize the connection between a sense of mystery and the senses of sight, hearing, touch and so on – the senses that make possible any engagement with the world.

The Book of Zhuangzi is packed with figures – craftsmen, butchers, farmers – who live in harmony with, and appreciation of, the *dao*. That it is figures like these, rather than scholars, who are chosen illustrates the Daoist emphasis on the primacy of practice over intellect. It is only because people know *how* to deal with things, situations and other people that they can progress to the cerebral knowledge *that* something is such-and-such. Spades, flutes and plants must first have their place in human practices in order to be identified *as* spades, flutes or plants. The Daoist craftsmen have an understanding of the *dao* in virtue of how they work, not because a treasury of philosophical truths is lodged in their heads. A wheelwright takes his noble employer to task for seeking the *dao* through reading books. True understanding, he rather bravely explains to his angry master, is found in what is 'felt in the hand' and 'from the heart'; it is something 'the mouth cannot put into words' (Zhuangzi 2009: Ch. 13). The idea that understanding is located and implicit in practices is the message, as well, that Zen masters give when they advise those in search of enlightenment to boil rice, chop wood or fetch water instead of reading Buddhist sutras.

Zhuangzi's wheelwright could just as well have been a gardener. Echoing the Chinese wheelwright's remarks, a distinguished English gardener writes that the essential knowledge that he and other practitioners of the craft possess comes through 'physical contact'; it is found 'through the hands [rather] than through the head' (Page 1995: 16). The words apply, too, to the enlightened understanding, and appreciation of the *dao* sought by those who follow the Way of the garden. Like the other Ways, gardening is a form of self-cultivation, of cultivating a life in which it becomes possible to feel and to follow the natural, *dao*-given flow of things. Because of its peculiarly close, 'hands on' engagement with the natural world, gardening is especially suited to achieve what all Ways seek to do.

Paul Cézanne did several portraits of his gardener, Vallier. Typically, they depict a serene figure entirely at home, whether working or sitting, in his garden. These paintings of Vallier depict a man very much in harmony with his environment, a man whose demeanour and comportment manifest humility, care for, and intimacy with the plants and trees that surround him. He epitomizes the virtues of the good gardener, of the person who authentically follows the Way of the garden. But, in his stillness, repose and gentle skills he manifests as well an understanding of nature and the way of things. Vallier is, as Martin Heidegger put it in a poem inspired by Cézanne's paintings, 'thoughtful' (in

Young 2002: 108). But this thoughtfulness is not deliberation or calculation; rather, it is the understanding of a man who, as he works, spontaneously responds to things, who implicitly appreciates the ways of plants, bees and fruit-bushes, and 'lets them be' what they are, tending to their needs.

If Vallier has a sense of the mystery of things, it is not because he has read books of spiritual edification and agreed with them. It is because, to use one of Heidegger's favourite terms, he 'dwells' in a certain way (Heidegger 1971). The garden, for Vallier, is not raw material that he must transform into something useful or easy on the eye. It is a place with a tone and mood, a context in which he belongs and is at home, an environment that is his theatre of meaning.

Vallier's awareness of the mystery of things belongs with his perception that this theatre of meaning – his garden, the place he 'dwells' in – is not of his, or anyone else's, making. This perception need not be 'dumb'. It is natural for someone, like Zhuangzi's wheelwright, whose experience cannot be articulated or explained in literal terms nevertheless to want to express it. Cézanne wrote that artists have a tendency to seek and find only themselves in their works. In their hubris, they fail to see that 'everything comes to us from nature; we exist through it'. Here he expresses in figurative words the same conviction that he communicates through paintings that depict a gardener who welcomes what 'comes to him', as if it were a gift.

That last word deserves its italics. For the man or woman who truly 'dwells' in a place, it has a certain tone or mood. This is the tone or mood, I want to say, of a place that is experienced as a gift.

GARDEN, 'GIFT', MYSTERY

The metaphor of the garden as the world in miniature is a rich one. It suggests, we noted, that the virtues of the good gardener are also those of the good person, of each citizen of the world. But it suggests, too, that moods and perceptions inspired by the garden transfer to the larger world. Zen gardens, it's been said, afford a revealing 'glimpse of this world as it appears to a Zen-enlightened sensibility' (Saito 1996: 59). I want to compare the sense of the world as the gift of a mysterious source with the sense of the garden as a gift.

The idea of a gift first appeared in Chapter 2. There the aim was to express or gesture at an alternative to viewing the world either as a fiction, an illusion, or as something 'objective', existing independently of our perspectives. It gestured at the idea of a world of experience that is the presencing for us – the gift – of what is ineffable. In the present chapter, the question is how a sense of the world as gift may be cultivated, deepened, firmed up. The proposal is that experience of the garden as gift is a way of doing this. The gardener who sees what he or she grows and tends as gift is at least close to receiving the world as a whole as something given forth.

That many gardeners do see their gardens like this is clear. For the poet and garden maker, Alexander Pope, the gardener should recognize that what grows there is given through a 'grace beyond the reach of art' (Pope 1994: 8). The same vocabulary is used by a more recent author when he describes the squash he grows as something 'given' him, a gift of 'grace' (Pollan 1996: 156). For these as for many other writers, talk of the garden as gift is also a call for humility, for appreciating the profound 'dependence' of gardeners on what is not in their 'own power to make'. Gardening, remarked Goethe, is 'voluntary dependence' (Goethe 1971: 195). But it's not just the poets – the Goethes and the Popes – who are sensitive to this dependence, this reliance on grace. The rhetoric is there in gardening magazines and in the words of ordinary gardeners when they try, often shyly and hesitantly, to convey what their gardens mean for them.

Very striking is the resilience of this sense of the garden as gift – its persistence in the face of concessions to 'common sense' that, at first sight, might seem to make nonsense of it. To understand this resilience is to understand why a sense of the garden as gift extends to a sense of the mystery of the world and its source.

The first thing that gardeners will of course admit is that success in growing squashes or sunflowers is due in part to elementary physical processes like photosynthesis and rainfall. But this scientific or naturalistic explanation of the plant's growth does nothing to impugn the feeling that it owes to grace and giving. 'The squash is a gift' isn't simply a figurative way of saying 'Well, the rain, the sun, the earthworms all contributed: it wasn't just me and my green fingers'. The reason, surely, is that it isn't just the squash, but the rain, sun, worms, and the rest of nature itself that are felt to be given. When the French philosopher, Gabriel Marcel, urges artists – gardeners included – to cultivate 'wonder' at what is 'granted to us as gift', his name for what grants it is not 'Nature', but 'Being' – his word for the mysterious source of everything, nature included (Marcel 2001: 32, 87). To go into your garden and feel compelled to describe what is before you as given, as a gift, is in effect to be on the edge of sensing the mystery of being.

There's a second thing gardeners, unless they are being falsely modest, will also admit – that it is due, not just to the sun and the rain, but to their own skills and patience that the squash and sunflowers turned out so well. So to experience the garden as gift is not to erase yourself from the process, to deny that you had anything to do with its flourishing. The gardener is not a passive recipient of a gift, but belongs with or among what is given. What the gardener is given is less like a gift out of a Christmas stocking than a gift for music or for friendship – something that is not separable from the person who has it and from this person's dealings with the world and other people. To experience the garden as gift is not only to have a sense of nature as gift, but of ourselves too as belonging to this gift. It is not just nature, but culture-and-nature – in effect, the whole world of experience – that is being felt as gift, as something that is received and to be enjoyed.

But a gift from whom or what? One merit of comparing the gift of the garden with a gift for music is that such questions are seen to be wrong-headed. Nobody and no thing, after all, gave Mozart his gift for music. When Zhuangzi compares the *dao*'s 'giving forth' with a festival's giving forth of blessings, he wants us to resist thinking of the *dao* as a person or thing, as something separate from what it gives (Zhuangzi 2009: Ch. 17). The festival is not a generous donor that dispenses blessings to people; it is a stretched-out event or 'happening' in and through which people feel blessed. That's how it 'gives forth'. The garden, music, nature, the world, us – the world, in effect – is a gift without a giver. The *dao*, the source of the world, is not an outside agent, separate from the world it gives; it is the entirely mysterious and constant 'happening' whereby a world comes to presence.

On an afternoon in autumn, we can imagine, a woman is in the garden that she made and tends, picking ripened fruit from a tree, perhaps, or watering a rose bush that is still in bloom. Birds fly into the garden, hoping to find some berries, and there are still bees on the buddleia. If she were asked, at this moment, how she felt about the garden she has known for many years, she would struggle for words. But 'gift' and 'grace' might well be among them. It's not the fruit tree or the rose bush taken separately, not even the garden that is contained within its walls, that she feels inclined to call a gift. The sense of gift extends beyond those walls, to the surrounding environment and still further, to the larger natural world on which the garden, like she herself, depends. If pressed to answer the question 'Whose gift?', she would resist giving an answer. For the experience of something as gift does not always point to a person or other being that supplied it. But the woman knows that in feeling compelled to describe her world as gift, she is acknowledging a mystery – the mystery of the source that is the giving forth of this world. It is an acknowledgement inspired by – perhaps compelled by – her long and intimate engagement with her garden. Hers has been the Way of the garden, a Way through which a sense of the mysterious ground of the world is cultivated.

REFERENCES

Cooper, D.E. 2006, *A Philosophy of Gardens*, Oxford: Oxford University Press.

Cooper, D.E. 2015, 'Gardeners of the Cosmos': The Way of the Garden in East Asian Tradition, in A. Giesecke and N. Jacobs (eds), *The Good Gardener?: Nature, Humanity and the Garden*, London: Artifice.

Goethe, J.W. 1971, *Elective Affinities*, London: Penguin.

Heidegger, M. 1971, Building, Dwelling, Thinking, in *Poetry, Language, Thought*, New York: Harper & Row.

Herrigel, G. 1999, *Zen and the Art of Flower Arrangement*, London: Souvenir.

Kasulis, T.P. 2004, *Shinto: The Way Home*, Honolulu: University of Hawai'i Press.

Keswick, M. 1980, *The Chinese Garden*, London: Academy.

Kirkland, R. 2004, *Taoism: The Enduring Tradition*, London: Routledge.

Marcel, G. 2001, *The Mystery of Being*, Vol ii, South Bend, IN: St Augustine's Press.

Page, R. 1995, *The Education of a Gardener*, Brighton: Harvill.

Pollan, M. 1996, *Second Nature: A Gardener's Education*, London: Bloomsbury.

Pope, A. 1994, *Essay on Man and Other Essays*, New York: Dover.

Saito, Y. 1996, Japanese Gardens, *Chanoyu Quarterly*, 83, 40–61.

Takei, J. and Keane, M. (tr.) 2001, *Sakuteiki: Visions of the Japanese Garden*, Boston: Tuttle.

Young, J. 2002, *Heidegger's Later Philosophy*, Cambridge: Cambridge University Press.

Zhuangzi. 2009, *Zhuangzi: The Essential Writings*, Indianapolis, IN: Hackett.

8

LIFE AND MYSTERY

ETHICS

A main theme of this book has been the relationship between senses of mystery and ordinary practices like walking and gardening. Openness to mystery is not disjoined from sensory and bodily engagement with the world. It is not found, primarily at least, in the motionless silence of contemplation or in ecstatic visions. It is through ordinary practices that a sense of mystery can be cultivated. And this is why we should expect a sense of mystery, once cultivated, to inform, shape and provide meaning to our everyday lives.

The implications of a sense of mystery for life is not an issue that I can legitimately ignore. The defence of mystery sketched in Chapter 2 was, in part, a pragmatic one that invoked our need for a measure of our lives. We cannot, I urged, accept that our convictions and purposes have no grounding or significance 'beyond the human' – that our own conventions and decisions provide the sole justification for them. To accept this is in effect to concede that our lives are without any grounding or measure. But the thought that there is no measure – that our lives are answerable to nothing whatsoever – is an unbearable one. It's the thought that nothing you do – writing a book, raising children, working in hospitals – matters any more than anything else you might have done. And this, in effect, is to think of your life as empty of meaning.

Since any world we can describe is 'a human world', not reality 'as such', then we cannot find in the world any objective measure of our convictions and values. So if there is measure at all, it must be sought in what is mysterious – in the ineffable source of everything we can describe and experience, in what 'gives' the world and indeed ourselves.

But how can what is impenetrable by language and thought provide guidance as to how we should live? To understand how, some preliminary remarks are needed on how the question of living well, of the good life, is addressed in traditions, like Daoism, on which I'll continue to draw.

The question of the good life belongs to ethics – but not to ethics as the term is usually understood in modern Western thought, as a synonym for 'moral theory'. The dominant approaches in Western moral philosophy, such as utilitarianism and rights theories, are very different from ancient reflections on the ethical. First, a divorce has now been effected between understanding and morality, between knowledge and virtue. It's taken that someone may know the world, understand how things are, but that a further and quite different kind of deliberation is required if he or she is to decide what is good or right. 'Ought', one is told, never follows from 'is'. Second, the focus of modern moral theories is squarely upon *action*. Typically, a moral theory attempts to identify a set of principles that determine the right thing to do in this or that situation. Finally, a sharp distinction gets drawn between the morally or ethically good and other kinds of goodness, such as beauty and friendship. These latter, we hear, are no doubt important pluses in life, but they are quite separate from, and subordinate to, the weightier considerations of right, duty and justice.

In all these respects, modern ethics or moral theory departs from ancient reflections on the good life. Aristotle's ethics, for example, consisted mainly in reflection, not on right action, but on virtues of character (*ethike arete*). For Aristotle, these can only be identified by first understanding how the world is. For the virtues are those aspects of character that enable people to flourish by realizing their *telos* – their place in the order of things and the goals that set them apart from everything else in nature. Nor would Aristotle have made any sense of the modern tendency to isolate and elevate a special group of 'moral' virtues, like respect for rights. For him, friendship – an ingredient, surely, in a flourishing life – belongs among the virtues as much as justice does (Aristotle 1999: Bk VIII).

Similar points apply to ethical reflection in Asian traditions. To live well, a person must understand the way of things: there exists a union of wisdom and virtue, not yet sundered by the modern divorce between knowledge and goodness. A person's task is to make his or her life responsive to the way of things, not to work out a system of principles, rights and obligations. For Daoists, indeed, an obsession with rules of conduct is a sure sign that people have 'lost the Way'. Were they properly attuned to the Way, the *Daodejing* explains, they would have no need to formulate principles of 'benevolence and righteousness' (Laozi 2003: Chs 18–19). Buddhists may place greater weight on 'precepts', such as those that forbid killing and lying. But while obedience to precepts – to *sīla* – is a significant component in the Eightfold Path to enlightenment, it would be wrong to equate Buddhist ethics with these injunctions. Of greater importance is mindful cultivation of the central virtues of compassion, loving-kindness, and the other so-called 'divine abidings' (*brahma-vihāra*) (see Buddhaghosa 1991: Ch. IX). If these are cultivated, there is no temptation to violate the precepts. The ethical life, for the Buddhist, is one informed by these virtues, each of which requires insight into reality – into, for example, the truths of 'not-self' and impermanence.

How a sense of mystery plays a role in these ancient spiritual traditions, I'll turn to in a moment. But we can already say that these traditions at least open up the possibility for mystery to play a role – in a way that modern Western moral theories do not. It's hard to imagine, for example, how the ineffable could be called upon to lend a hand in the business of establishing systems of rights. The idea of mystery does not have its place in systematic moral theorizing, but in a different style of ethical reflection.

REMOVING OBSTACLES

Let's imagine some people in whom a sense of mystery has been cultivated, in whom the thoughts that the world is mysterious, that the emergence of a world is mysterious, and that there is a mysterious source of things, have gone deep. What difference might this make to their lives? What might they now recognize as virtues? What practices will they feel attracted or compelled to adopt?

No doubt the very practices – gardening, perhaps – that had helped them to cultivate a sense of mystery will continue to attract them. This is less because of a therapeutic need to keep in spiritual trim than because, implicit in these practices, are precisely the virtues that are consonant with a sense of mystery. We'll see shortly what some of these virtues are, but first we need to identify some attitudes or postures that are *obstacles* to recognition of these virtues, and indeed to the sense of mystery itself. People in whom a sense of mystery is already cultivated will want to guard against relapsing back into these attitudes and to help others overcome them.

These tasks are not easy, for the postures that threaten a sense of mystery are entrenched in modern society. To begin with, there's what might be labelled the 'existentialist' or 'humanist' posture. This sits easily with the idea, discussed in Chapter 2, of the world as a fiction or construction, as a human world beyond which there is nothing at all, mysterious or otherwise. It's the posture of those for whom the only possible measure of values, meanings and purposes is human convention and commitment. We are answerable to nothing but ourselves, to the decisions we have made in exercising a freedom unconstrained by anything beyond ourselves. From this standpoint, the moral hero is some-one who freely 'chooses' and resolutely commits to a particular way of living.

This posture not only excludes a sense of mystery but, in its celebration of choice and commitment, is scornful of just the kind of attunement to things that, we've seen earlier, nurtures a sense of mystery. A distinguished writer on nature describes the importance for him of '"fitting" . . . [of] going with the flow' of natural life. He recalls how 'disorientating' – how much of a 'block' – he had found a philosophical posture that urged him to impose his individual stamp on the world, rather than to adjust and respond to its flow (Mabey 2005: 75). The gardeners, walkers and musicians we have encountered would sympathize with his recollection.

Next, there's what I'll call the 'theoretical' posture – a com-panion to the scientific image of reality discussed in Chapter 2. People adopting this posture assert, to begin with, that reality 'as such' is not at all mysterious and can, in principle, be fully described and conceptualized. They then claim that this will be the achievement of *theory*, of scientific theory in particular. Our ordinary, everyday image of the world, they say, may indeed be hopelessly perspectival, but it is one that should be replaced, for purposes of serious enquiry, by the scientific image. The person whose life should be admired is someone who is devoid of the sentiments that accompany everyday experience of things, who is instead coolly objective, yet dedicated and industrious in establishing the scientific truths on which decisions should be based. If, for example, science shows that familiar moral feelings are simply the spin-off of natural selection – of the doings of 'selfish' genes – then they are emotions that should not have any authority in the making of hard-headed decisions.

Here, again, is a posture that not only denies the existence of mystery, but militates against sentiments that promote or reflect a sense of mystery. For example, it is hardly the posture of people who feel that the world is a 'gift' since, according to it, there is nothing besides the world as science describes it of which that world could be a gift. Nor would there be any sympathy for the feeling that some animals may 'look out into the Open' and hence be 'in the truth'. On the 'theoretical' posture, animals, since they are innocent of theory, know nothing – nothing, that is, true of reality 'as such'.

Finally, there is a posture – the 'technological' one – that is an unholy alliance of elements of the first two postures. While the world cannot be both a human construct and the objective one of the sciences, it is possible, as we well know, to put science at the service of a Promethean, 'existentialist' urge to impose a purely human measure upon the world. The result of this alliance is the transformation of nature, without sentimental scruples, into 'equipment' or 'standing-reserve' at the disposal of human beings (Heidegger 1977: 15ff). We shouldn't worry, for example, when animals are cloned or genetically engineered if, as some biologists tell us, an animal is merely 'a vehicle for genes' that it is legitimate to shunt around. The moral heroes, according to the 'technological' posture, are the 'Faustian' figures described by Oswald Spengler: engineers, industrial farmers and others who represent 'the victory of technical thought' in the exercise of human 'will to power' (Spengler 1932: 84).

The 'technological' posture of course excludes a sense of mystery and, once more, is inimical to perceptions of the natural world that encourage this sense. Intent on the urgent, muscular pursuit of fixed technological goals, 'Faustian Man' is hardly prone to 'revery', to a relaxed and flexible mindfulness of the world around him. Instead, his world is ordered and regimented by the imperatives of technology. Again, someone whose perception of an animal is that of a 'vehicle for genes' is incapable of the meditative walker's experience of natural beings as 'gathering' whole environments, as beings that owe their identity to their place in rich and integrated networks. It was a related 'technological' perception, perhaps, that was responsible for something I encountered on a walk yesterday: a heap of ten piglets piled up by the side of a country lane. For some farmer these little creatures had presumably become redundant, superfluous.

One important way, then, in which a sense of mystery will inform someone's life will be to inspire this person to renounce and resist the postures I have been describing. They are ones that impugn, occlude or otherwise deny access to any sense of mystery.

HUMILITY AND COMPASSION

But does a sense of mystery encourage something more positive than resistance to the postures that impugn it? What virtues – what ingredients of living well – might it endorse? It helps, in answering these questions, to distinguish two ways in which a sense of mystery encourages recognition of something as a virtue. Soon I'll discuss the ancient thought that a way of living is virtuous because it *emulates* the mysterious way of things. First, though, I ask which ways of living are especially *consonant* with a sense of mystery. Which ones, that is, would be naturally embraced by a person with this sense? Such a person does not have to perform a feat of deduction; he or she doesn't need to infer from the mystery of things how to act and feel, rather their actions and attitudes will spontaneously flow from their sense of this mystery.

The postures described in the previous section have something striking in common: each of them is hubristic, each in its way is arrogant, vainglorious. The 'existentialist' posture is that of people arrogant enough to imagine that their lives are answerable to nothing beyond their own decisions, that they are themselves the sole measure of goodness and meaning. The 'theoretical' posture is a catalogue of hubristic attitudes: a condescending treatment of ordinary perceptions of the world; a dismissal of accounts of the world alternative to that of the favoured theory; and the pretence that human beings can rise above their perspectives so as to arrive at an absolute account of reality 'as such'. The 'technological' posture adds to this hubristic cocktail the conviction that it is a legitimate purpose to put theoretical knowledge at the disposal of those who aim to shape and exploit the natural world according to their whims.

The virtue that stands opposed to the vice of hubris is humility. Better, perhaps, this is a set of closely related virtues that share an appreciation of the necessary limits on what people, individually or collectively, have the capacity to understand, judge and accomplish (see Kidd 2016). They are virtues discernible in the practices – like gardening and meditative walking – described in earlier chapters. But we need to make them explicit and understand their consonance with senses of mystery.

A feature of several of the figures engaged in the various practices I described was a willing readiness to offer recognition to and respect for things and creatures. The person authentically engaged with animals, for example, not only affirmed that animals do have perspectives, but that these may be radically different from any human one without therefore being stunted or distorted. The gnat's world that Nietzsche imagined is as genuine as a human one. This is a recognition and respect that should extend to the perspectives of human cultures very different from our own. That the world of the hunter-gatherer, say, might be very unlike the world that we moderns experience is no ground for regarding it as impoverished. Or, recall the meditative walker's appreciation of the integrity of things – of a tree, a pond, a rock. This was, in effect, a recognition and respect for what a thing itself is – of its place in rich environmental networks.

In all these cases, humility is a form of 'unselfing', a refusal to regard and judge creatures, people or things from within the narrow compass of one's prejudices and perspectives. It is a style of humility that is adopted by someone in whom a sense of mystery has been cultivated. For it is an implication of the truth of mystery that the compass of any human perspective, however entrenched and taken for granted it may be, is indeed narrow. Openness to the idea that different worlds mysteriously emerge from a ground that is itself mysterious allows a person to see that there is hubris in the privileging of narrow perspectives that blot out the existence of other ways of revealing things. Humility of recognition and respect is the virtue that flows from this concession.

Another feature of figures from Chapters 4–7 was their appreciation of the dependence not only of their, but of humanity at large's, achievements and creations on what is not of human making, on what is 'given' to us. The composer, performer and hearer of music comes to recognize the mutual inflections – the inter-dependence – between musical experience and engagement with nature. Gardeners know that the success of their endeavours owes not just to the cooperation of a local environment, but to the gift of nature itself. Implicitly they are recognizing their dependence on what Pure Land Buddhists call 'other power' (*tariki*), and the corresponding arrogance of people who imagine themselves to be autonomous beings, super-charged with 'self-power' (jiriki). For it is not only our achievements, but we ourselves – as ingredients in the world of experience that comes to presence – that are dependent. Humility, wrote Gabriel Marcel, is 'a mode of being incompatible with the claim that we have the power to make ourselves, dependent only on ourselves'; instead, it involves appreciation of our capacities as graced and gifted to us (Marcel 2001: 87).

A life infused by a sense of mystery will therefore be one in which the humility of dependence is practised and deepened. The poetic expression of this humility is that of the world, including ourselves, as a gift. Not a gift that is separate from the giver; 'other power' is not the possession of a potent divinity, a creator god, but – to continue in the poetic idiom – the arising of worlds from a mysterious well-spring. Here then are virtues – those of humility – that are consonant with the truth of mystery. When practised, they help to cultivate a sense of mystery that, in turn, is drawn upon to confer a tone of humility on the conduct of life itself.

There's another virtue – the pre-eminent Buddhist virtue – that is especially consonant with a sense of mystery. The call to be compassionate to all beings is not, for the Buddhist, some precept bolted, as an afterthought, onto an understanding of reality. Rather, it is a virtue that will be naturally exercised by whoever has properly absorbed this understanding. Someone genuinely 'endowed with knowledge of emptiness', a Mahayana text tells us, will then 'course in the perfection of morality' (Conze 1979: 535). This is because the vices of 'greed, aversion and delusion' drop away or atrophy once their basis in a wrong-headed conception of the world – as a receptacle of substances and selves – is eroded.

I called compassion 'another' virtue, but it is closely allied to the virtues of humility. For, to erode the ground on which greed and other vices stand is, in effect, to discredit the postures – like the 'technological' one – that constitute hubris. People who, in their humility, refuse to impose their stamp and purposes upon creatures and things are at the same time viewing these with compassion. The sufferings of animals, after all, mean little to people for whom they are simply 'vehicles for genes' or, like the heaped-up piglets, lumps of matter to dispose of if they become unprofitable. We are freed up for compassion when the world about us is no longer hubristically regarded as a reservoir of things to cater to our greed, no longer as 'my possession', in Dōgen's words, but as the gift of 'something ineffable coming like this'. Zen masters like Dōgen do not exhort themselves to be compassionate. They have no need to, since compassionate regard for things is interfused with their sense of, their insight into, the source of things.

EMULATION

From a sense of mystery, then, flows a recognition of the virtues of humility and compassion. Consonant with this sense, they belong in a life that is led well. But mention of Zen masters prompts reflection on a further way in which a sense of mystery serves to identify virtues and the meaningfulness of a life. The virtuous life is not only consonant with the truth of mystery, but may *emulate* the mysterious way of things.

In many religious traditions, importance and honour are attached to certain exemplary figures – the sages and 'consummate' persons of Daoism, for example, or the masters and bodhisattvas of Mahayana schools of Buddhism. A main reason for their prestige is precisely the mystery, the ineffability, of the truths into which such figures are deemed to have insight. If the truth of things cannot be 'said', then it might nevertheless be 'shown'. And one way it is shown is through the life – the comportment, bearing, gestures, demeanour – of the exemplary figure. As we saw in Chapter 3, it is confidence in such figures that is a main form of faith in some traditions. Faith in the truth of their words derives from the confidence invested in these persons.

A striking claim made in these traditions is that the sage or other exemplary person not only possesses a sense of the mystery of things, but that his or her life emulates this mystery. Indeed, it is precisely this emulation that renders the sage's life an exemplary one. The rest of us, in turn, bring virtue and significance into our own lives by trying to emulate the sage. This kind of claim, however foreign it may sound to the modern Western ear, is not unfamiliar in Western traditions. Drawing on Plato's own view, later Neo-Platonists argued that the ultimately real, the One, is devoid of material features and that the good person is one whose life becomes more *like* the One through abandoning sensuality and other bodily entrapments. In Christianity, the attempt to emulate God can tip over into heresy; nevertheless, a familiar thought among artists of the Middle Ages and the Renaissance was that their creative labour emulated, however modestly, the Creation itself.

But the clearest instances of traditions that embrace the idea of virtue as emulation are found further East. Especially clear is the Daoist conception of the sages as people who, in exercising the paramount virtue of spontaneity (*ziran*), emulate or 'embody' the *dao* itself. This is because, as the *Daodejing* teaches, 'the *dao* is itself modelled on what is spontaneous' (Laozi 2003: Ch. 25).

Spontaneity, or 'naturalness', was a quality of some of the figures we met with in earlier chapters – the musician who 'jams' with the sounds of nature, for example, or the meditative walker, like Bashō, whose journeys had 'no rules'. It emerged from such examples that the virtue of spontaneity is not that of behaving capriciously, according to whim. Nor, of course, is this the sense in which the *dao* itself is spontaneous; it is not some playful, whimsical divinity. The *dao* is 'self-so'; it is unconstrained by anything outside of it and has nothing to contend with, nothing it needs to impose itself upon. The sage, analogously, is not caught up in webs of rules, conventions and external diktats; nor, as Zhuangzi tells us, is he 'a repository of plans and schemes' that determine his actions and feelings. The sage's way with people, animals and things is a gentle one: confrontation and contention are avoided. The sage's virtues are those of responsiveness, flexibility, 'following along with the way each thing is', and 'conducting his affairs through non-action' (wu wei) (Zhuangzi 2009: Chs 5 and 7).

But there's more to emulation of the dao than this. The dao is the source of all things, what gives a world and everything contained in it. It confers identity on each thing and, through the rhythms of nature of which it is the source, it 'nurtures' things, enabling them to flourish. So when Zhuangzi tells us to 'follow along with the way each thing is', he doesn't mean that the sage should simply leave everything alone. In addition, the sage is – to recall an earlier metaphor – 'a gardener of the cosmos', 'nourishing' and caring for things. To exercise the virtue of spontaneity is not only to refrain from contention and imposition, but to respect the 'self-so-ness' of creatures, and to nurture 'the myriad things in their natural condition'. Sages emulate the dao by letting living things be – not through simply leaving them to their own devices or fates, but through helping them to realize their lives. In doing so, they themselves become realized human beings. Like the men and women from Chapter 4 whose relationship to animals was a genuine 'being with', the Daoist sage is not 'separated off from the creatures of the world' and does not ignore their 'views of right and wrong'. Instead, the sage is mindful of and responsive to the nature of the pig or the horse, refusing to submit the creature to human 'plans and schemes'.

The dao, emptiness, or however one labels the well-spring of everything, is mysterious, ineffable. The language just used in connection with the dao – non-contending, spontaneous, giving and so on – is indelibly figurative. But it is not absurd for someone with a sense of this mystery to reflect on how a human life might nevertheless emulate the way of things. Perhaps, though, it is less a matter of reflection than of response. The Daoist sage and Zen master do not have to agonize at length about how their lives might chime with this mystery. How this life should go is felt with the same spontaneity that is one of the main virtues of this life.

So, a sense of mystery may inform and guide our lives. Mystery lends measure and meaning to these lives; they are lives both answerable and appropriate to mystery. Humility, compassion, spontaneity . . . these and other virtues are, through consonance or emulation, marks of lives that respond to mystery.

REFERENCES

Aristotle. 1999, *Nicomachean Ethics*, Indianapolis, IN: Hackett.

Buddhaghosa. 1991, *The Path of Purification*, Kandy: Buddhist Publication Society.

Conze, E. (tr.) 1979, *The Large Sūtra on Perfect Wisdom*, Delhi: Banarsidass.

Heidegger, M. 1977, *The Question Concerning Technology and Other Essays*, New York: Harper & Row.

Kidd, I.J. 2016, Intellectual humility, confidence and argumentation, *Topoi*, 35 (2), 395–402.

Laozi. 2003, *The Daodejing of Laozi*, Indianapolis, IN: Hackett.

Mabey, R. 2005, *Nature Cure*, London: Chatto & Windus.

Marcel, G. 2001, *The Mystery of Being*, Vol ii, South Bend, IN: St Augustine's Press.

Spengler, O. 1932, *Man and Technics*, London: Allen & Unwin.

Zhuangzi. 2009, *Zhuangzi: The Essential Writings*, Indianapolis, IN: Hackett.

9

IN A GARDEN AGAIN

The book began with my late afternoon walk around a Sri Lankan garden. It was a walk, I liked to think, that offered me glimmers, intimations, of mystery. This was a reason why walking in a garden could be an example of ordinary activities that help to cultivate senses of mystery. After sketching a defence of the truth of mystery, and relating the idea of mystery to religious sensibility, I went on to describe some of these activities. They were ones through which, by engaging with nature, a sense of mystery is fostered. Finally, I addressed the question of how a sense of mystery, once cultivated through these practices, might inform our lives and provide measure and meaning for them.

I had intended that the book would end with another walk around a garden; the same garden, perhaps, but by a different person – someone who, unlike myself, was fully attuned to the mystery of things. My intention was to describe the walk in the words of such a person. I found myself wanting to put words like these into his or her mouth:

> I am slowly walking down the steps of a garden . . . It is still light, but soon it will be dark . . . This light is reflected by the surface of a pool and by the scales of the small red fish that swim just below its surface . . . I can hear the calls and chatter of birds . . . and the soft sounds of a solitary flute . . . As I climb back up the steps, the light has already faded. The little world around me is becoming shadowy, its contents indistinct . . .

If you turn back to the opening page of this book, you'll see that these words are identical with the ones I wrote to describe my own walk. So was I, after all, a person fully attuned to the mystery of things? No. But the fact that someone who is might use the same words as mine shows something else that is important. It suggests that this person's experience does not differ from mine because it is punctuated by mystical visions or feats of inner contemplation. There is 'nothing special' of that kind in the experience. The sage, as we might call this person, does not have experiences in addition to, or alongside, those I had. The sage's sense of mystery pervades an experiential engagement with the garden, its creatures and environment. It is not tacked on to this engagement; rather, it is diffused over the ordinary activity of walking around a garden.

That the sage's words are the same as my own suggests that the difference between our experiences cannot be articulated in a set of literal propositions, any more than the mystery the sage is attuned to can be. The difference, I want to say, is in the *tone* that the garden – and, indeed, the world as a whole – has for the sage, the *key* in which it is experienced.

But how does this differ from my more fragile and stuttering intimations of mystery in the garden?

Well, this way of putting the question provides part of the answer to it. There is a constancy, an abidingness, to the way the world presents itself to the sage. The experience of mystery is not, as it is for me, one that flickers on and off. Another part of the answer is that, for the sage, intimations of mystery are entirely spontaneous. He or she does not need to adjust their vision or hearing for the world to figure for them in the key of mystery. But this can't be all that there is to distinguish the sage's experience of the garden from mine, for we have yet to get a feel for what the tone or key of the world might be like for the sage.

It helps to recall the earlier metaphor of the 'double exposure' performed by the enlightened Buddhist who experiences as 'one Reality' both 'the world of particular objects' – trees, ponds, deer – and the 'suchness' that is their ineffable source. At one level, this experience is no different from yours or mine; it's the same set of particular objects that both of us might encounter on a walk. But, at another level, everything is changed; for the enlightened person, the objects are charged with meaning, transparent to the source from which they mysteriously emerge.

If we are to get a feel for what this experience of meaning and transparency is like, we must resort to analogy with experiences that, hard as they may be to describe, are at least more familiar to us. Consider, for example, the strange but undeniable transition in the way a person may hear a piece of music. The notes are no different, but now the piece is heard with understanding; they fit together in a coherent whole, with phrases pointing forwards or backwards to other passages. The music has become meaningful even though nothing about it has changed. And further sense may be made of it when it is heard transparently, as it were: when one hears through it to its source, to what it expresses. It is heard, say, as an expression of nostalgia for the composer's motherland, or as an attempt to come to terms with a loss of religious faith. And at once everything about the piece then falls into place. The music is now heard as having a different tone, as being, metaphorically, in a new key. Nothing about the music has changed, yet everything has.

Or think of the delicate transition that takes place when two people come to recognize that their friendship has become a relationship of love. Neither person has altered; they look the same, do the same, say the same. But each figures for the other in a changed key. A familiar gesture is now perceived as an expression of care, a shared hobby as a ritual of communion, a holiday together as a symbol of mutual dependence. Everything in the relationship takes on a fresh hue, tone and significance for the two people. And they become transparent to each other; they see through the gestures, the words, the shared jokes, the presents they exchange to the love that they now know to be the source of all of this.

These transitions can occur, too, in experience of places, including gardens. What was once just a space in which to mow the overlong grass, or sunbathe with a gin-and-tonic at hand, one day becomes a place in which to *dwell*. Benches, birds and bushes take on a meaning they previously lacked. And if the owner of the garden is at all like the gardener imagined at the end of Chapter 7, it will have become transparent, for he or she will see it as a gift – will, as it were, see through it to the source that made it possible.

To know what it is like to be attuned to mystery, you need already to be attuned to it. The rest of us, with our paler and more intermittent intimations of mystery, must get a feel for it in other ways. By reflecting, for example, on analogies with other forms of experience where things or people or places come to figure in a new key. And more crucially, of course, by engaging in practices, like those on which this book has focused, that help to foster a sense of mystery.

INDEX